150 Ways to Enjoy Potatoes

by
Dr. Duane R. Lund

Including
Recipes • Preparation Tips • Soups
and Sweet Potato Recipes

Distributed by
Adventure Publications, Inc.
P.O. Box 269
Canbridge, MN 55008

ISBN 1-885061-85-4

150 Ways to Enjoy Potatoes

First Printing, January 2000
Second Printing, September 2000

Printed in the United States of America
by
Nordell Graphic Communications, Inc.
Staples, Minnesota 56479

Dedication

To R.D. Offutt

He transformed agriculture in Central Minnesota, where
the POTATO now is king!

His technology has enhanced the quality of this popular
vegetable and as a result you and I can enjoy the 150
recipes in this book even more.

TABLE OF CONTENTS

SECTION III
BAKED/ROASTED POTATOES

SECTION IV
SKILLET POTATOES

HASH RECIPES

SECTION V
MASHED POTATOES

SECTION VI
POTATO CASSEROLES

SECTION VII
POTATO CAKES AND DUMPLINGS

SECTION VIII
MISCELLANEOUS RECIPES

SECTION VIX
SWEET POTATOES

Sweet Potatoes with Pecans and a Touch of Orange */97*
Mellow Sweet Potatoes */97*
Sweet Potato Wedges */98*
Sweet Potato French Fries */98*
Sweet Potatoes with Cheese */98*
Senator Richard Russel's Sweet Potatoes */99*
Sweet Potato Strips with Lime */99*
Sweet Potato Pecan Pie */99*
Sweet Potatoes with Bacon */100*
Sweet Potato Soup */100*

Section I
POTATO SOUPS

CREAM OF POTATO SOUP

Ingredients to serve 6:

4 medium potatoes, quartered
1 medium onion, peeled and chopped
2 ribs of celery, chopped
2 medium carrots, chopped
2 cups chicken broth
2 cups milk
1/2 t salt
1/4 t pepper (use white if available)
2 T chopped parsley for garnish

Combine all ingredients except milk in a soup pot. If the broth does not cover the solid ingredients, add enough water to cover. Bring to a boil, then reduce heat to simmer for about 20 minutes or until vegetables are tender. Let cool until safe to handle.

Process or blend in batches until smooth.

Return to kettle; add milk and heat until piping hot - but do not let boil.

Garnish with chopped parsley.

As an option, process or blend only half the ingredients; leave the rest as solids.

POTATO SOUP WITH ONION, CELERY AND GARLIC

Ingredients to serve 4:

2 cups potatoes, peeled and chopped quite fine
1 small onion, chopped fine
2 rib celery, chopped fine
1 clove garlic, chopped fine
3 medium leeks, chopped (both white and green parts)
1 small carrot, sliced thin (optional)
1/4 pound butter or margarine, melted (1 stick) or 8 T oil
2-1/2 cups chicken broth

1/2 cup cream

1 t poultry seasoning

2 T chopped parsley (either stir into soup or use as garnish)

Melt butter and sauté potatoes, onion, celery, carrot and garlic for a few minutes or until onion pieces are translucent. Add leeks and all other ingredients except parsley. Cook over low heat until potatoes are soft. Serve hot. Either stir in parsley or use as a garnish on surface.

POTATO SOUP WITH CORN

Ingredients to serve 6:

2 medium potatoes, chopped

1 carrot, chopped

2 cups fresh corn (may substitute whole kernel in the can)

1 clove garlic, minced

1/4 pound butter or margarine (1 stick) or 8 T oil

2 ribs celery, chopped

1 small jar pimentos

1/2 t basil

2 T chopped green pepper

4 cups chicken broth

1 t poultry seasoning

salt and pepper to taste

Using the melted butter, sauté the onion, green pepper and garlic a few minutes until onion is translucent. Add corn and potatoes and continue to sauté until potatoes are soft. (If corn is already cooked, do not sauté). Add other ingredients except broth. Continue to heat and stir about 2 minutes. Add broth; let simmer 20 minutes or until all vegetables are soft.

DEER CAMP POTATO SOUP

Ingredients to serve 8:

5 potatoes (medium), peeled, cooked and diced

2 ribs celery, chopped

2 carrots, sliced thin

1 large onion, chopped

2 cloves garlic, minced

3 T flour

1/8 pound butter or margarine (1/2 stick) melted, or 4 T oil

1-1/2 quarts milk

1/2 t basil

1/2 t thyme
1 bay leaf
2 chicken or beef bouillon cubes
1/2 t salt (to taste)
1 t pepper (to taste)
1/4 pound cheddar cheese, grated and shredded (as garnish)

Cook potatoes in salted water until easily penetrated with a fork. Sauté the celery, onion, carrots and garlic in melted butter a couple of minutes or until onion is translucent. Stir in flour and slowly add milk. Add all other ingredients except cheese and potatoes.

Cook about 20 minutes (stirring regularly) or until soup starts to thicken.

Add the pre-cooked, diced potatoes. Simmer another 20 minutes or until piping hot. Remove bay leaf. Spoon shredded cheese on top of each serving.

QUICK AND RICH POTATO SOUP

Ingredients to serve 6:

1 medium onion, chopped
2 ribs celery, chopped
1 clove garlic, minced
3 cups chicken broth
3 cups potatoes, peeled and diced
2 cups half and half or heavier cream
1/2 t oregano
1/2 t pepper
chopped chives or parsley for garnish

In a soup pot, place all the ingredients except the cream. Bring to a boil then reduce heat and cook for 15 to 20 minutes or until potatoes are soft. Add the cream and continue to cook until piping hot but do not let boil. Serve with choice of garnish.

If you prefer, you may purée the soup before you add the cream. Let cool first, however, so that the soup may be handled safely.

POTATO SOUP WITH SPINACH

Ingredients to serve 4:

2 medium potatoes, peeled and diced
2 cups frozen spinach (or fresh leaves) packed
1 onion, peeled and chopped
3 cups water

1 cup milk
1/2 t curry powder
salt and pepper to taste
garnish with 4 t chopped chives

Cook the diced potatoes and onion in the water until soft (15-20 minutes).

Meanwhile, chop the spinach (unless frozen is already chopped).

Let potatoes cool. In a blender, purée potatoes (with water) spinach and onion. Return to soup kettle and add all other ingredients except chives. Bring to a boil, then reduce heat to simmer for 20 minutes. Garnish with chives.

MASHED POTATO SOUP WITH BACON

Ingredients to serve 8:

5 medium potatoes, peeled and diced
10 strips bacon, cut into half-inch pieces
3 ribs celery, chopped
1 large onion, peeled and chopped
4 T flour
4 cups chicken broth
4 cups milk
2 cups sour cream
salt and pepper to taste (white pepper if available)

Fry bacon bits in a soup pot until crisp. Set bacon aside for garnish.

Sauté the celery and onion in the bacon grease until onion is clear.

Add the potatoes and the broth. Cover and cook until potatoes are tender (about 20 minutes).

Mash about half of the potatoes with a large spoon; this will help thicken the soup.

Stir the flour into the sour cream. Add the sour cream and the milk to the pot; stir thoroughly.

Continue to cook until piping hot but do not let boil.

Garnish each bowl with the bacon bits.

BAKED POTATO SOUP #1

Ingredients to serve 8:

5 medium baked potatoes (skin may be left on) diced
1 medium onion, chopped
2 ribs celery, chopped

1 clove garlic, minced

1 cn. cream of chicken soup

1 cn. cream of celery soup

2 cns. water

1 cup cream

1/8 pound butter or margarine (1/2 stick) or 4 T oil

1/4 pound cheddar cheese, shredded or grated

salt and pepper to taste

Bake potatoes, let cool, cut into small chunks.
Sauté the onion, celery and garlic in the melted butter a few minutes or until onion is translucent. Combine all ingredients (except cheese) in a soup pot. Simmer over low heat for 20 minutes; do not boil. Serve soup piping hot with cheese on surface as garnish.

BAKED POTATO SOUP #2

Ingredients to serve 6:

6 large baked potatoes

1 large onion, peeled and chopped

2 cns. Chicken broth

6 slices bacon fried crisp and broken into bits

2 cups water

1 cup heavy cream

6 T shredded or grated cheddar cheese

salt and pepper to taste

Bake the potatoes and fry the bacon in advance. Sauté the chopped onion in the bacon grease (or cooking oil) a couple of minutes or until onion is clear.
Scoop the potatoes out of the skins and mash.
Combine all ingredients except the cheese in a soup pot. Bring to a boil, then reduce heat to simmer and cook for another 15 minutes.
Serve with a sprinkling of cheese on top of each bowl.

POTATO WITH TOMATO

Ingredients to serve 6-8:

5 medium potatoes, peeled and diced

3 cns. Italian style tomatoes

1 onion, chopped

2 ribs celery, chopped

2 cloves garlic, minced

2 bay leaves
1/2 cup cream
1/2 t sage
1/2 t oregano
1/8 pound butter or margarine (1/2 stick) or 4 T oil
2 T catsup
enough water to cover potatoes plus 4 cups
parsley or celery leaves for garnish

In the melted butter, sauté onion, celery and garlic a few minutes until onion is translucent.

In a soup pot, cover the chopped potatoes with water and cook (boil) until potatoes are soft. Discard water. Add all other ingredients (including 4 cups of water and liquid in cns. of tomatoes) and bring to a boil. Reduce heat immediately and let simmer about 10 minutes.

Remove bay leaves. Serve piping hot.

Garnish with parsley or celery leaves.

POTATO SOUP WITH CARROTS AND A HINT OF ORANGE

Ingredients to serve 6:

2 large potatoes, peeled and diced
4 carrots, sliced thin
2 cns. chicken broth
2 cns. water
1 orange (juice of and rind grated)
1 bay leaf
1 T brown sugar
1 cup cream
1 t Tabasco sauce
salt and pepper

In a soup pot, combine the diced potatoes, sliced carrots, chicken broth, water, sugar, Tabasco and bay leaf. Bring to a boil, then reduce heat to simmer and cook for 20 to 30 minutes or until vegetables are tender. Let cool to handle safely. Remove and discard bay leaf. Add the grated orange rind and juice.

Purée the soup in batches; return to kettle.

Add cream and re-heat until piping hot but do not let boil. Season to taste.

POTATO SOUP WITH HAM

Ingredients to serve 8:

5 large potatoes; peeled and diced
1-1/2 cups diced, pre-cooked ham
6 cups chicken broth of stock
2 onions, peeled and chopped
4 T butter, margarine or oil
3 leeks, sliced, including green parts
1 bay leaf
1 cup cream
1/2 cup white wine
1 t coriander
salt and pepper to taste
chopped chives for garnish

Sauté the onion and leeks in the butter for a few minutes until translucent. Place in a soup pot with all ingredients except the ham, cream and wine. Bring to a boil, then reduce heat to simmer and cook for 30 minutes or until the potatoes are soft. Let cool for safe handling. Remove bay leaf.
Add wine and cream and purée. Return to soup pot, add the diced ham and re-heat (do not let boil).
Serve with chopped chives for garnish.
(Small strips of fried bacon may be substituted for the ham).

POTATO SOUP WITH BROCCOLI

Ingredients to serve 6:

1 onion, chopped
2 clove garlic, minced
1 rib celery, chopped
1/8 pound butter or margarine or 4 T oil
2 carrots, sliced thin
2 cups broccoli, cut bite-size
2 cups diced potatoes
4 cups chicken broth
salt and pepper to taste
1/2 t curry powder
chopped chives for garnish

Sauté the onion, garlic, carrots and celery in the butter until onion is translucent. (do not let burn) Place in a soup pot.
Add all other ingredients and bring to a boil. Reduce heat and simmer until carrots and potatoes are tender.
Garnish each bowl with chopped chives.

POTATO AND CORN CHOWDER

Ingredients to serve 6:

1 onion, chopped
2 strips bacon, cut crossways into narrow strips
1 rib celery, chopped
2 large potatoes, peeled and diced
2 cns. whole kernel corn (Mexicorn if available)
1 cn. chicken broth
1 cn. water
2 cups milk
2 T flour
salt and pepper to taste
parsley flakes (or chopped fresh) for garnish

Place the chopped bacon in the bottom of a soup pot over medium heat. As soon as grease appears, add chopped onion and celery. When bacon is crisp, add chicken broth, potatoes and water. Bring to a boil, then reduce heat to simmer for 20 minutes or until potatoes are soft. Stir the flour into about a half cup of milk, then add this mixture plus the rest of the milk to the pot. Continue to heat (do not boil) for about 5 minutes or until piping hot.
Season to taste.
Garnish with parsley.

NEW ENGLAND CHOWDER

Ingredients to serve 8-10:

2 pounds skinned fish fillets, deboned and cut into chunks
3 onions, sliced and broken into rings
4 large potatoes, peeled and cut into bite-size pieces
3 cups water
5 T salt
10 peppercorns
2 carrots, chunked
1 quart milk
2 cup cream

Bring the water to boiling. Add all ingredients except the fish, milk and cream. Bring to a boil and continue boiling until the potatoes and carrots are done. Stir in the milk and cream, add fish, bring to a boil, reduce heat and let simmer, covered 20 minutes.

LONG ISLAND CLAM CHOWDER

Ingredients to serve 6:

4 medium potatoes, peeled and diced
3 ribs celery, chopped
2 carrots, sliced thin
1 medium onion, peeled and chopped
1 bottle (8 oz.) clam juice
3 6 oz. cans of minced clams; use liquid also
4 medium tomatoes, diced
1 t thyme, dried
salt and pepper to taste
oyster crackers

Combine all ingredients except clams and tomatoes in a soup pot. Bring to a boil, then reduce to simmer and cook until vegetables are tender (about 20 minutes).
Add tomatoes and clams and continue to heat for another 5 minutes or until piping hot.
Serve with oyster crackers.

SMOKED FISH SOUP

Use either saltwater or freshwater fish

Ingredients to serve 6:

2 pounds smoked fish (remove bones)
4 potatoes, peeled and cut into bite-size chunks
2 medium onions, peeled and chopped
salt to taste (other seasonings may be added, such as white pepper, thyme, dill or your favorite)
2 T parsley, chopped
4 T butter, margarine or oil
3 cups cream
parsley, chopped, for garnish

Cover the potato chunks with water and boil until done. Meanwhile, sauté the onion in the butter. Using the pan in which you sautéed the onion, add the potatoes, cream and seasonings. Simmer (do not boil) until all ingredients are hot. Serve in shallow bowls over pieces of smoked fish and garnish with the chopped parsley.

SPLIT PEA SOUP WITH POTATOES

Ingredients to serve 8:

1/8 pound butter or margarine, melted (1/2 stick) or 4 T oil
1 onion, peeled and chopped
2 ribs celery, chopped
2 carrots, chopped
1 pound dry split peas, rinsed
3/4 pound ham, cubed bite-size
7 cups water
2 chicken bouillon cubes
2 medium potatoes, peeled and cubed
1 t tarragon
1 t Beau Monde
1 t poultry seasoning
salt and pepper to taste
croutons for garnish

Sauté the onion and celery in the melted butter a few minutes until onion is translucent. Combine all ingredients in a soup pot and simmer 1-1/2 hours (or longer if vegetables are not tender).
Garnish with croutons.

POTATO SOUP WITH BEETS
(AMERICANIZED RUSSIAN BORSCHT)

Ingredients to serve 6:

3 medium potatoes, peeled and cubed
3 medium beets, diced
1 medium onion, chopped
1 rib celery, chopped
3 cups chicken broth
1 cup half and half
2 T flour
2 T oil
1 T dried, crushed spices of your choosing. You might try basil, tarragon and/or rosemary. Total spices: 1 T
Garnish with chopped chives.

Sauté the onion and celery in oil until onion pieces are clear (2 or 3 minutes). Stir in flour.
Combine onion and celery in a soup pot with the potatoes, beets, chicken broth and spices. Bring to a boil, then reduce heat to simmer and cook covered for about 20 minutes or until potatoes are tender. Let cool until it can be safely handled.
Process or blend the mixture in batches until smooth.
Return to the kettle; add the cream. Re-heat but do not boil.
Garnish with chopped chives.

POTATO SOUP WITH A KICK!

Ingredients to serve 6:

4 medium potatoes, peeled and diced
1 medium onion, peeled and chopped
2 ribs celery, chopped
2 cloves garlic, minced
4 cups chicken stock
1 cup sour cream
3 T oil
1/2 cup vodka (or more if you dare!)
salt and pepper (preferably white) to taste
3 T chopped chives for garnish

Sauté the onion, celery and garlic in the oil in a soup pot a few minutes or until onion is clear.

Add all ingredients except the vodka, chives and sour cream. Cover and bring to a boil, then reduce to simmer and continue cooking for about 20 minutes or until the potatoes are very soft.

Crush the potatoes (with a large spoon) against the bottom and sides of the pot.

Stir in the sour cream and the vodka. (If you want to avoid the alcohol, add the vodka before boiling the potatoes.)

Garnish with chopped chives.

Section II
POTATO SALADS

POTATO DINNER SALAD

Ingredients to serve 6:

6 new red potatoes, sliced with skins on
1 medium red onion, peeled, sliced thin and broken into rings
1/2 cup olive oil
2 T vinegar
1 t oregano
1 t rosemary
2 tomatoes, cut into wedges
4 cups lettuce leaves, torn
1 cup cheddar cheese, shredded, grated or diced

Cook the potatoes in water in a sauce pan, covered, about 20 minutes or until soft.

In a small bowl, whisk together the liquid ingredients to make a dressing. Place all other ingredients in a large bowl and gently toss as you gradually add the dressing.

DINNER POTATO SALAD WITH BEETS

Ingredients to serve 6-8:

4 medium potatoes, peeled and cut into half-inch chunks
4 medium beets (a little smaller than the potatoes) cut into half-inch chunks
1 medium onion, peeled, sliced thin and broken into rings
1 cup sweet pickle relish
a dressing of your choosing

Cook the potato and beet chunks (separately), covered for 15-20 minutes until soft.

Let cool (refrigerate). Combine all ingredients.

Options:
1. 1-1/2 cups of diced, cooked ham
2. Substitute pickled beets for cooked beets

POTATO AND FISH DINNER SALAD

Ingredients to serve 6:

2 cups cooked and diced potatoes
2 cups cooked and diced beets
1/2 cup flavored vinegar of your choosing
1 cup chopped sardines or similar oily fish
2 T chopped onions
1 cup mayonnaise
3 T tartar sauce
6 large lettuce leaves
fresh ground pepper to taste

Combine all ingredients and refrigerate at least 30 minutes.
Arrange a large lettuce leaf (or a couple of small ones) on each salad plate. Spoon the salad onto the lettuce leaves.

POTATO SALAD WITH DILL

Ingredients to serve 6:

12 small new potatoes, sliced (with or without skins)
1 medium onion, peeled, sliced thin and broken into rings
4 T diced green sweet pepper
4 T diced red sweet pepper
3 T chopped fresh dill
1/2 cup olive oil
3 T lemon juice or vinegar
1/2 cup sour cream
pepper to taste
garnish with paprika

Boil the potatoes in a covered sauce pan for about 20 minutes or until done.
Gently combine all ingredients. Refrigerate at least 30 minutes before serving.

POTATO SALAD WITH BEATEN EGGS

Ingredients to serve 6-8:

12 small, new red potatoes, sliced, with or without skins
1/2 cup olive oil
1/2 cup vinegar of your choosing
2 large eggs (or 3 small) beaten*
1 cup sugar

1 T flour
1 t ground mustard
1/4 t pepper
4 green onions, white parts only, chopped
4 T water

Boil the potatoes in a covered sauce pan for 20 minutes or until done. Refrigerate 30 minutes.

Combine sugar, flour, water, mustard, vinegar, salt, pepper and oil in a sauce pan. Bring to a boil then reduce heat. Stir until mixture begins to thicken. Combine dressing with potatoes, onions and beaten eggs. Refrigerate at least 30 minutes.

There is a health risk when using raw eggs.

POTATO SALAD WITH HAM

Ingredients to serve 6:

8 medium new potatoes, diced (if red variety, leave skin on for color)

2/3 pound cooked ham, diced into bite-size chunks (a little less than 2 cups)

1/3 pound shredded or diced cheese of your choosing (I like Swiss with ham)

1/2 cup vegetable or olive oil

1/2 cup wine vinegar

2 T Dijon mustard

4 shallots or green onions sliced thin (white part only)

1/4 cup chopped almonds

1/2 t salt

1/4 t pepper (I like white)

4 T chopped parsley for garnish

lettuce leaves (serve on lettuce leaves)

Cook the diced potatoes in water in a covered sauce pan for about 20 minutes or until soft. Refrigerate 30 minutes.

Use half the vinegar, oil and mustard to coat the potatoes (toss gently in a bowl). Refrigerate 20-30 minutes.

Toss the rest of the oil, vinegar and mustard with the remaining ingredients (except the parsley and lettuce leaves).

Combine with potatoes; garnish with parsley; serve on lettuce leaves if you wish.

POTATO SALAD WITH ASPARAGUS

Ingredients to serve 6-8:

10-12 medium red potatoes, sliced or diced (skins on)
3/4 pounds fresh asparagus, cut into bite-size pieces, cooked
2 T Dijon mustard
3 shallots or green onions, sliced thin, white parts only
2 ribs celery, chopped
1/2 cup sour cream
3 T vegetable or olive oil
3 T lemon juice or vinegar
1/2 t salt
1/4 t pepper
1 t thyme
1 t rosemary
3 T chopped parsley for garnish

Cook the sliced or diced potatoes with water in a covered sauce pan and boil for about 20 minutes or until soft. Refrigerate at least 30 minutes.

Cover the asparagus pieces with water in a sauce pan. Bring to a boil, then reduce heat to simmer until tender (about 12 minutes). Refrigerate at least 30 minutes.

Combine all ingredients in a large bowl, including the asparagus, and gently toss. Serve with parsley garnish.

A good quality mayonnaise may be substituted for the oil and lemon juice.

POTATO SALAD WITH FRESH GARDEN PEAS

Ingredients to serve 4:

8 small potatoes, sliced (if new and red, leave skin on)
1/2 cup sugar
2 T olive or vegetable oil
2 T vinegar or lemon juice
1-1/2 cups fresh, garden peas
4 slices bacon, fried crisp and crumbled

Boil the sliced potatoes until tender (about 20 minutes, covered). Refrigerate 30 minutes.

Place the peas in a sauce pan of boiling water for about one minute; remove and let cool.

Combine all ingredients gently. Refrigerate for about 30 minutes.

POTATO SALAD WITH ZUCCHINI

Ingredients to serve 6:

10 small potatoes, sliced or diced
1 small to medium zucchini, sliced thin (raw or pre-cooked)
3 ribs celery, chopped
2 cups salad greens, torn or chopped
3 eggs, hard-boiled, cooled and sliced thin
1 small purple onion, sliced and broken into rings
3 T chopped parsley
1/2 t salt
1/4 t pepper
1/2 cup plain yogurt or sour cream
3 T Dijon mustard
3 T olive oil or mayonnaise
1 T sugar

Cook sliced or diced potatoes in water in a covered sauce pan for about 20 minutes or until soft. Refrigerate 30 minutes.

Cook the eggs in boiling water at least 5 minutes, cool, peel and slice.

Make a dressing by combining the last four ingredients.

Combine all ingredients in a large bowl and gently fold in the dressing. Serve at room temperature or refrigerate for about 30 minutes.

POTATO SALAD WITH BITS OF BEEF

Ingredients to serve 6:

10-12 small, new potatoes, sliced or diced
2 cups left-over roast beef, diced
3 T chopped onion
2 ribs celery, chopped
4 T chopped sweet red or green pepper or 1/2 of each
3 T prepared horseradish
4 T vegetable or olive oil
3 T vinegar or lemon juice
3 T chopped parsley for garnish
1/2 t salt
1/4 t pepper

Cook the sliced or diced potatoes in water in a covered sauce pan for 20 minutes until soft. Refrigerate 30 minutes.

Blend the oil, vinegar, horseradish, salt and pepper. Combine all ingredients (except the parsley) in a large bowl and then gently fold in the dressing until everything is well coated.

Sprinkle on the parsley and serve. May be refrigerated before serving - about 30 minutes.

POTATO SALAD WITH BACON, WALNUTS AND POPPY SEEDS

Ingredients to serve 6:

10 small to medium potatoes, sliced or diced
1 small onion, sliced and broken into rings
3 ribs celery, chopped
6 slices bacon, fried crisp and crumbled
2 cups salad greens
1/2 cup walnuts, chopped
4 T olive or vegetable oil
3 T poppy seeds
2 T lemon juice or cider vinegar
3 T apple juice or cider
1 clove garlic, minced

Cook the sliced or diced potatoes in a covered sauce pan for 20 minutes or until done. Refrigerate 30 minutes.

Fry bacon until crisp; cool and crumble.

Make a dressing of the last five ingredients. Place all other ingredients in a bowl and gently fold in the dressing until everything is coated.

Bacon bits may be used as a garnish or folded into the salad.

GERMAN STYLE POTATO SALAD #1

Ingredients to serve 6-8:

10 medium red potatoes, sliced or diced
4 ribs celery, chopped
1 medium to large onion, peeled, sliced and broken into rings
3 hard boiled eggs, sliced or cut into wedges
8 bacon strips, fried crisp and broken into bits
2 T vinegar
2 T vegetable oil
3/4 cup sour cream
1/2 t salt
1/4 t pepper
3 T flour

Using a sauce pan, cover the sliced or diced potatoes with water and cook covered until done (about 20 minutes).

Fry the bacon strips in a skillet until crisp. Let cool and break into bits. Save the drippings.

Make a dressing by combining the last six ingredients plus 2 T bacon drippings.

Combine all ingredients and gently fold in the dressing. The bacon bits may be used as a garnish or folded into the salad.

Serve hot; this may necessitate re-heating in a skillet or using a microwave.

GERMAN STYLE POTATO SALAD #2

Ingredients to serve 6:

10-12 small potatoes, sliced or diced
6 strips bacon, fried crisp then broken into bits
1 medium onion, sliced and broken into rings
1/2 cup wine or cider vinegar
1/2 t salt
1/4 t pepper
3 t chopped parsley for garnish

Using a sauce pan, cover the sliced or diced potatoes with water, then cook covered - 20 minutes or until done.

Using a skillet, fry the bacon until crisp. Let cool. Remove bacon and break into bits. Save 2 T of the bacon drippings.

Sauté the onion in 2 T bacon drippings a couple of minutes or until the onion is clear.

Place everything in the skillet. Stir gently over low-medium heat until all ingredients are warm (do not let burn).

Garnish with parsley or stir into the salad.

GERMAN STYLE POTATO SALAD #3

Ingredients to serve 6-8:

10-12 small, new potatoes, peeled, sliced or diced
1 medium onion, peeled, sliced and broken into rings
3 ribs celery, chopped
1/2 cup chopped sweet green pepper
6 bacon strips, fried and broken into bits
1 T prepared mustard
3 T cider or wine vinegar
3 T lemon juice
1 T flour
1/2 t salt
1/4 t pepper

Using a covered sauce pan, cover the sliced or diced potatoes with water and cook 20 minutes or until soft.

Fry the bacon in a skillet until crisp. Remove, let cool then break into bits.

Using the bacon drippings, sauté the onion, green pepper and celery a couple of minutes or until onion is clear.

Remove all but 2 T of the bacon drippings; add the potatoes and keep warm over low heat.

Prepare a dressing of the last 6 ingredients (whisk together). Fold the dressing into the contents of the skillet, coating everything uniformly. Serve hot with bacon bits as garnish or stirred into the salad.

ITALIAN STYLE POTATO SALAD

Ingredients to serve 6:

12 small new red potatoes, sliced or diced
8 anchovies, drained and chopped
1 small head of lettuce, torn into bite-size chunks and pieces
1/4 cup grated Parmesan cheese
1 clove garlic, minced
4 T seasoned Italian dressing
4 T olive oil
2 T lemon juice

In a covered sauce pan, cover the sliced or diced potatoes with water and then cook about 20 minutes or until soft.

Place the lettuce pieces in a large salad bowl.

Place the oil in a skillet. Add the anchovies and minced garlic. Sauté a couple of minutes.

Add the potatoes, Italian dressing and lemon juice to the skillet. Stir constantly as you continue to heat (low-medium). After 5 minutes, pour the contents of the skillet over the lettuce. Toss gently. Stir in the Parmesan. Serve immediately.

MEXICAN STYLE POTATO SALAD

Ingredients to serve 6-8:

10 small new potatoes, sliced or diced with skins on or off
1 sweet red pepper (small), seeded and chopped
3 T chopped jalapeno peppers (use kitchen gloves)
1/2 cup black beans, drained
2 ribs celery, chopped
1 small to medium red onion, sliced and broken into rings
2 T chopped fresh cilantro or parsley
1 cup cubed or shredded Monterey Jack cheese
1/2 cup salsa, your choice of how hot
1/2 cup spicy Italian dressing
1/2 t salt
lettuce leaves (to serve on)

Cook the potatoes in water in a covered sauce pan for 20 minutes or until soft.

Combine the salsa and Italian dressing.

Combine all ingredients (except lettuce leaves) in a large bowl. Fold in the dressing, gently, until everything is coated.

May be served hot or cold on lettuce leaves.

POLISH STYLE POTATO SALAD

Ingredients to serve 6:

8-10 small new potatoes, sliced or diced
3 cooked Polish sausages, sliced in half-inch chunks
2 ribs celery, chopped
1 medium onion, peeled and sliced and broken into rings
4 T chopped parsley, either mix with salad or use as garnish
2 T flour
2 T sugar
2 T prepared mustard
1/2 cup wine vinegar
1/2 cup olive or vegetable oil

Cook the sliced or diced potatoes in water in a covered sauce pan until tender (about 20 minutes).

Cover the sausages with water and cook in a covered sauce pan. Bring to a boil; remove from heat; keep covered for 5 minutes. Let cool. Slice into half-inch chunks.

Sauté the celery and onion in the oil for a few minutes until onion is clear. Add flour, mustard, sugar and vinegar. Continue to heat and stir until it starts to thicken.

Combine all ingredients and gently fold in the dressing until everything is covered.

Serve hot. If necessary, warm a few minutes in a large skillet. Stir occasionally; do not let burn.

POTATO SALAD WITH SHRIMP #1

Ingredients to serve 4:

8 small potatoes, sliced or diced
1 pound shrimp, cooked, peeled and deveined
1 medium onion, peeled, sliced and broken into rings
2 ribs celery, chopped
2 T lemon juice
3 T chopped parsley
1 cup sour cream or mayonnaise
1/2 t salt
1/4 t pepper (I prefer white)
1 T Dijon mustard

Place the shrimp in a bowl and drizzle with the lemon juice. Gently stir until well coated.

Cook the potatoes (peeled, sliced or diced) in water in a covered sauce pan for about 20 minutes or until soft. Refrigerate 30 minutes.

Make a dressing by combining sour cream (or mayonnaise), mustard, salt and pepper.

Place all ingredients in a large salad bowl. Gently stir in the shrimp and dressing.

Serve cold. (Refrigerate 30 minutes if you wish)

POTATO SALAD WITH SHRIMP #2

Ingredients to serve 4:

8 small potatoes, peeled, sliced or diced

1 pound shrimp, cooked, peeled and deveined

4 green onions or shallots, sliced (white parts only)

2 tomatoes, cut into wedges

2 cups of lettuce, torn into bite-size pieces

1/2 cup mayonnaise

1/2 t salt

1/4 t pepper (I prefer white)

Cook the sliced or diced potatoes in water in a covered sauce pan for about 20 minutes or until tender. Refrigerate 30 minutes.

Combine all ingredients in a large salad bowl and gently fold in the mayonnaise. If everything is not coated, use a little more mayonnaise.

Serve at room temperature or refrigerate 30 minutes and serve cold.

POTATO SALAD WITH SALMON

Ingredients to serve 6:

8-10 small, new potatoes, sliced or diced

1 pound salmon fillet, pre-cooked

2 T lemon juice

1 cup asparagus, cooked and cut into 1 inch pieces

3 ribs celery, chopped

1 medium onion, peeled and sliced and broken into rings

6 cups salad greens

1/2 t salt

1/2 t lemon pepper

3/4 cup mayonnaise

1/2 t thyme

1/2 t tarragon

Cook the peeled and sliced or diced potatoes in water in a covered sauce pan for about 20 minutes or until soft. Refrigerate 30 minutes.

Cut the asparagus into one inch pieces and cook in water in a covered sauce pan about 12 minutes or until tender. Let cool.

Season the salmon with salt and pepper and bake in alumafoil in a 350° degree oven for about 10 minutes. Do not over-cook. When it flakes easily with a fork it is done. Let cool. Break salmon into small pieces and place in a bowl. Drizzle the lemon juice over the fish and stir gently to coat.

Combine all ingredients in a large salad bowl and gently fold in the mayonnaise. If all parts are not coated, use more mayonnaise.

Refrigerate 30 minutes.

POTATO SALAD WITH WINE

Ingredients to serve 6:

6 medium potatoes, cut into wedges (bite size)
6 green onions, sliced, white parts only
1/2 cup white wine
1 T olive oil
salt and pepper to taste
parsley garnish

Cover the potato wedges with water and boil 12 to 15 minutes or until soft (test with a fork). Drain.

Place potatoes in a serving bowl and sprinkle with wine and oil and toss, adding a little salt and pepper to taste.

Serve hot or cold.

POTATO SALAD ON THE GRILL

Ingredients to serve 4:

6-8 small potatoes, sliced or diced
1 medium carrot, sliced thin
1 medium onion, peeled, sliced and broken into rings
2 ribs celery, chopped
1/2 sweet green pepper, seeded and cut into strips
1/2 sweet red pepper, seeded and cut into strips
4 slices bacon, fried and broken into bits
6 cups salad greens
1 clove garlic, minced
4 T butter or margarine
1/2 t salt
1/4 t pepper
1/2 cup olive or vegetable oil
1/2 cup vinegar

Cook the sliced carrots and potatoes (sliced or diced) in water in a covered sauce pan for 10 minutes or until they just start to soften.

Fry the bacon in a skillet until crisp. Let cool and break into bits.

Make two "pockets" from alumafoil. Place equal portions of butter, potatoes, carrots, green and red pepper strips, onion rings and celery into each pocket. Sprinkle a little pepper, salt and minced garlic into each pocket. Seal the pockets with your fingers and place on a hot grill. Cook for about 15 minutes.

Place the salad greens and bacon bits in a large salad bowl. "Dump" the contents of the foil pockets into the bowl (use gloves). Gently fold in the oil and vinegar.

Serve hot.

OLD FASHIONED POTATO SALAD

Ingredients to serve 6:

6 medium to large potatoes
1 medium sweet onion, sliced and broken into rings
2 ribs celery, chopped or sliced thin
3 hard boiled eggs, chopped or sliced thin
1 cup mayonnaise
1/2 cup sour cream
3 T red wine or wine vinegar
3 T sugar
2 T mustard (prepared)
salt and pepper to taste (Don't be shy with the pepper)

Boil the potatoes about 15-20 minutes or until done. (Test with a fork). Let potatoes cool, then slice or cube.

Combine all ingredients, then toss. Refrigerate several hours before serving.

QUICK AND SIMPLE POTATO SALAD

Ingredients to serve 4:

8 small potatoes, sliced or diced
2 ribs celery, chopped
1 medium onion, peeled, sliced and broken into rings
1/2 cup mayonnaise
1/4 cup water
2 T dried salad dressing mix
3 T chopped parsley

Cook the sliced or diced peeled potatoes in water in a covered sauce pan for about 20 minutes or until tender. Drain and refrigerate 30 minutes.

Whisk together the mayonnaise, water and dressing powder.

Place the potatoes, celery, parsley and onion in a salad bowl and gently fold in the dressing.

Serve at room temperature or refrigerate 30 minutes.

Section III
BAKED/ROASTED POTATOES

BAKED WHOLE POTATOES, SKINS ON

It is likely that humans first enjoyed potatoes baked in the coals and ashes of a campfire. And that is still a very special way to prepare potatoes. The coals and ashes somehow impart a unique flavor - even through the skin.

Today, potatoes are usually baked in an oven or on the grill. Microwave Cooking saves a great deal of time, but the flavor isn't quite the same and there is the danger of the ends of the potatoes being tough.

When baking potatoes in the oven or on the grill, select large potatoes of uniform size and thickness. Any variety will taste good, but I prefer russets.

Metal skewers will help cook the potatoes more quickly; alumafoil wrapping seems to bake them more uniformly.

Rubbing the outside skin with vegetable or olive oil before baking enhances the appearance and makes the skins themselves more palatable. However if you are going to stuff the potatoes, do not rub with oil as you want the skins to be tough so they won't tear.

Prick the potatoes with a fork before baking to prevent an explosion!

Per-heat the oven to 375°. I prefer the middle rack. Test with a fork after one hour.

TOPPINGS FOR BAKED POTATOES

There are so many possibilities! Pick and choose from those listed. Keep "presentation" in mind as well as added flavor.

butter or margarine (somehow, cold pats seem more flavorful)
bacon bits
ham, diced small
sausage, crumbled and fried
pimentos, chopped
onion, chopped
celery, chopped very fine
shallots, chopped (use either white or green parts or both)

chives, chopped
cheese (most any variety, grated or shredded)
sour cream
yogurt
dressings, seasoned
mushrooms, chopped
nuts, chopped fine
sweet peppers, chopped or small strips (green or red)
paprika
salt, regular or seasoned (including garlic)
pepper, fresh ground
parsley, chopped
jalapeno peppers, chopped (handle with kitchen gloves)
tomatoes, chopped

BAKED POTATOES STUFFED WITH VEGETABLES

Ingredients to serve 4:

4 large, baked potatoes
1/3 cup cooked carrots, chopped
4 T chopped jalapeno peppers (use kitchen gloves)
12 oz. jar pimentos, chopped
salt and pepper to taste
1 cup shredded or grated cheddar cheese

Cut the baked potatoes in half—lengthwise. Scoop out the "meat" and mash well.
Combine all other ingredients except the cheese and salt and pepper. Mound the mixture into the empty potato shells. Sprinkle with cheese and salt and pepper to taste.
Bake in a pre-heated 350° degree oven for 30 minutes.

BAKED POTATOES STUFFED WITH SALMON

Ingredients to serve 4:

4 large baked potatoes
1 medium onion, peeled and chopped
3 T butter or margarine, melted
1 pound fresh salmon, poached, de-boned and flaked
1 T Worcestershire sauce
1 cup sour cream
chopped dill for garnish

Poach the salmon in boiling water about 10 minutes or until it flakes easily with a fork.

Cut the baked potatoes in half-lengthwise. Scoop out the "meat" and mash well.

Sauté the chopped onion in the butter a few minutes until clear. Combine all ingredients well and heap into the potato shells. Bake in a pre-heated 350° degree oven for 30 minutes. Serve with butter.

TWICE BAKED POTATOES

Ingredients to serve 6:

6 medium to large russet potatoes
6 T butter, softened, two portions
1/2 cup sour cream
1/2 cup milk
1 cup fresh herbs of your choosing (possibilities are thyme, rosemary, basil, dill, chives, etc.)
1/2 t salt
1/4 t pepper

Pre-heat the oven to 375°. Prick potatoes with a fork. Place on middle shelf and bake. Test with a fork after 1 hour.

Let cool until safe to handle. Cut in half length-wise. Scoop out the potatoes, leaving about a quarter inch shell. Meanwhile, leave oven on. Mash the potatoes, working in half the butter (3 Ts). Blend in the milk.

Brush the insides of the potato skins with the remaining butter. Place them on a cookie sheet and return to the middle tray in the oven. After 20 minutes they should be a golden-brown color and fairly crisp. Check after 12-15 minutes so they do not burn.

Meanwhile, cut or chop the fresh herbs into small pieces. Work about 3/4 or the herbs and salt and pepper into the mashed potatoes.

Bring the shells out of the oven and fill each with the mashed potatoes, sprinkling the remaining 1/4 of the herbs on the top of the potatoes.

Return the potatoes to the oven for about 10 minutes to heat them through. It's all right if the potatoes get a little brown, but don't let them burn.

Serve with a dopple of sour cream on top of each half. Also, consider items listed in the introduction to this section.

BAKED MASHED POTATOES WITH EGG YOLKS

Ingredients to serve 6:

6 large potatoes, peeled and chunked
2 egg yolks
3/4 cup half and half
1/2 cup parmesan
1 stick butter or margarine, melted
salt to taste (about 1/2 t)

Cover the potato chunks with water in a sauce pan; boil for about 20 minutes or until easily penetrated with a fork. Drain and return to the stove for a couple of minutes to dry.

Mash together all ingredients except the parmesan. Spoon potatoes, evenly, into a lightly greased baking dish or pan (about 12x12). Sprinkle with the parmesan cheese.

Place on the middle shelf of an oven pre-heated to 375°. Remove when top is lightly browned (about 12-15 minutes).

POTATO SKIN HORS 'D OEUVRES

Ingredients to serve 6-8:

6 medium-large russet potatoes

4 T butter, melted

1 cup cheddar cheese, shredded or grated

1 cup chives, chopped or green onions, chopped very fine

1 sweet green or red pepper, seeded and chopped fine

5 slices bacon, fried crisp and broken into bits

1 t hot sauce - such as Tabasco

Pre-heat the oven to 375°. Prick potatoes with a fork and place on middle shelf of oven. Check for doneness with a fork after one hour.

Meanwhile, fry the bacon until crisp and break into bits; cool.

Remove potatoes from oven and let cool to handle. Scoop out the potatoes and save for some other purpose, leaving the shells about 1/4 inch thick. Cut each half in to halves or quarters.

Combine the melted butter with the hot sauce and brush the insides of each potato shell. Place under a broiler for a few minutes until crisp; watch closely; do not let burn.

Combine the cheese, chives, pepper and bacon bits. Place equal portions in each potato half. Return to broiler for just a minute or two until cheese melts.

Serve warm. This recipe may call for more hot sauce than you will like. The first time you make these, use a little less.

Option: Substitute salsa or pizza sauce for the hot sauce.

ZESTY ROASTED POTATOES

Ingredients to serve 6:

8 medium-large potatoes cut into chunks (with or without skins on)

2 T spicy Italian dressing

3 T olive oil

1/2 cup Dijon mustard

1 clove garlic, minced

Combine all ingredients except the potatoes. Place the potato chunks in a large bowl and stir in the sauce until potatoes are all coated.

Place potato chunks in a lightly greased flat baking dish or pan large enough so that the chunks can spread out and not be on top of each other.

Place in a pre-heated 375° oven, on the middle shelf. Roast about 45 minutes or until the potatoes are done (test with a fork). Stir the chunks every 15 minutes while roasting.

ROASTED ONIONS AND POTATOES

Ingredients to serve 6:

8 medium potatoes cut into chunks, with or without skins on

3 sweet onions, cut into a little smaller chunks

4 T butter, melted

1/3 cup olive oil or vegetable oil

3 T spicy Italian dressing

1/2 pkg. onion soup mix

Combine all ingredients in a large bowl and stir until all parts are coated. Drain any left-over liquid into the bottom of a flat baking dish or pan (large enough so potatoes and onions won't have to be on top of each other).

Bake in a pre-heated 375° oven for one hour or until potatoes are done; test with a fork. I prefer to use the middle shelf.

Stir every 15 minutes while baking.

ROASTED POTATO WEDGES

Ingredients to serve 4:

4 medium potatoes, cut into wedges, with or without skins on

4 T olive or vegetable oil

2 T minced, fresh herbs of your choice (basil, thyme or rosemary are all possibilities)

1/2 t salt

1/4 t pepper

Combine all ingredients in a bowl and stir until potato wedges are all coated.

Place in a lightly greased flat baking dish or pan (big enough so wedges are not on top of each other)) in a pre-heated 375° oven. Use the middle rack.

Test for doneness after 1 hour (with a fork). Wedges should be brown, but do not let burn.

BAKED SMALL RED POTATOES

Ingredients to serve 6:

16 small red potatoes (assuming 4 per guest; vary number with size of potatoes)

4 T olive oil

1/2 cup chopped fresh herbs, such as basil, thyme or rosemary

1 t salt

1/2 t black pepper

Combine all ingredients except potatoes. Using a large bowl, toss potatoes in the mixture until they are well coated.

Place in a lightly greased flat baking dish or pan in a single layer. Bake in a pre-heated 375° oven on the middle rack for 45 minutes or until done; check with a fork.

BAKED "FRIES"

Ingredients to serve 4:

5 large potatoes of your choice, cut into French fry type sticks (You may substitute a 32 oz. pkg. frozen fries)

1 cn. Cream of Mushroom soup

1/2 pound cheddar or American cheese, diced

1 medium onion, peeled and chopped fine

1 cup milk

2 T flour

salt

Peel the potatoes and cut them into French fry type sticks. Or use a pkg. frozen fries, thawed.

In a sauce pan, place the milk, cheese, onion, flour and soup. Cook over medium heat (do not let boil) until cheese melts and dissolves. Stir almost continually.

Place potato sticks in a lightly greased flat baking dish or pan - in a single layer. Pour mixture over sticks. Place in a pre-heated 375° oven for about 50 minutes or until tender. Sprinkle lightly with salt before serving.

MASHED POTATOES BAKE

Ingredients to serve 6:

6 large potatoes, peeled and quartered

4 T butter, melted, divided into 2 portions

1 small onion, peeled and minced

1 clove garlic, peeled and minced

1/2 cup sour cream

4 oz. cream cheese, softened

1/2 t salt

Parmesan cheese

Place the quartered potatoes in a sauce pan, cover with water and boil covered until tender (about 20 minutes). Drain and mash in a bowl, working in the onion, garlic, sour cream, cream cheese, salt and half the butter.

Place potatoes in a lightly greased baking dish or pan. Choose a size that will result in a layer of potatoes about 2 inches thick.

Sprinkle with remaining melted butter, then sprinkle lightly with Parmesan cheese (grated). Place in a pre-heated 375° oven, middle rack, for about 45 minutes.

BAKED MASHED POTATOES WITH GARLIC AND MUSHROOMS

Ingredients to serve 6:

6 large potatoes, peeled and quartered

2/3 cup sour cream

1/3 cup milk

1 pkg. (8 oz.) cream cheese

1 clove garlic, minced fine

1 stick butter (quarter pound)

4 T chives, chopped

6 T mushrooms, chopped

1/2 t salt

1/4 t pepper

Place the quartered potatoes in a sauce pan, cover with water and boil about 20 minutes or until tender. Drain and place in a large bowl.

Mash while working in all ingredients except the butter. Ingredients may blend easier if the sour cream, milk and creamed cheese are first blended with a mixer.

Place in a casserole and dot with pats of butter. Bake one hour, covered. Remove cover for another 10 minutes.

SLICED POTATOES BAKED IN WINE

Ingredients to serve 4:

4 large potatoes, peeled and sliced

4 slices bacon, fried or broiled and broken into bits

1 cup cheddar cheese, shredded or grated

1/2 cup chicken broth

1/2 cup white wine

salt and pepper

4 T chopped chives for garnish

Arrange the sliced potatoes, over-lapping but in layers in a lightly greased baking dish. As each layer is completed, sprinkle with all ingredients except the broth and wine. When the last layer is in place, drizzle the broth and wine over-all.

Bake, uncovered in a pre-heated 375° oven for one hour or until potato slices are tender. Garnish with chives before serving.

BAKED POTATOES O'BRIEN

Ingredients to serve 6-8:

1 pkg. frozen hashbrowns-about 2# (thaw out)

1 cn. cream of chicken soup

1 cup sour cream

4 T butter or margarine (melted) or vegetable oil

1 medium onion, peeled and chopped

1/2 sweet green pepper, seeded and chopped

1/2 sweet red pepper, seeded and chopped

1-1/2 cups cheddar cheese, grated or shredded

In a large bowl, combine all ingredients, stirring the potatoes in last. Place in a lightly greased flat baking dish or pan (about 10" x 12") Bake in a pre-heated 350° oven for 45 minutes.

BAKED HASH BROWNS

Ingredients to serve 6-8:

1 32 oz. pkg. frozen hash browns, thawed

3 T melted butter

1-1/2 cups cheddar cheese, shredded or grated

1 cup sour cream

1 cn. cream of mushroom soup

1 medium onion, peeled and chopped

salt and pepper to taste

bread crumbs

Combine all ingredients except salt, pepper, bread crumbs and melted butter. Spoon into a lightly greased baking dish or pan (about 10" x 12"). Lightly season with salt and pepper. Sprinkle generously with bread crumbs. Drizzle the melted butter over all.

Place in a pre-heated 350° oven and bake for 45 minutes.

BAKED SLICED POTATOES WITH CHEESE AND PARSLEY

Ingredients to serve 6:

6 large potatoes or 8 medium, peeled and sliced
1 stick (1/4 pound) butter or margarine, melted
1 cup grated or shredded cheese of your choosing
3 T fresh parsley, chopped
1/2 t dried rosemary or other dried herb of your choosing
2 T chopped onion
salt and pepper to taste

Layer the potatoes in a lightly greased, flat baking dish or pan. Drizzle the melted butter over the potatoes and then sprinkle with rosemary. Lightly season with salt and pepper. Cover and bake in a pre-heated 375° oven for 45 minutes to 1 hour or until potatoes are soft. Remove cover and sprinkle cheese evenly over potatoes. Return to oven, uncovered, until cheese melts (10-15 minutes).

Sprinkle with parsley flakes before serving.

BAKED HASHBROWN BREAKFAST

Ingredients to serve 6:

1 32 oz. pkg. frozen hashbrowns, thawed
12 large eggs
1-1/2 cups milk
2 cups pre-cooked ham, diced
2 T chopped green pepper
2 T chopped red pepper
4 T chopped onion
1-1/2 cups cheddar cheese, grated or shredded
1 small (4 oz.) cn. mushrooms
salt and pepper to taste

Spread the hashbrowns over the bottom of a lightly greased baking dish or pan (about 10" x 12").

Combine all other ingredients (except cheese, salt and pepper) and pour over the hashbrowns.

Season lightly with salt and pepper. Sprinkle the cheese uniformly over the surface.

Bake in a pre-heated 350° oven, covered, for 30 minutes. Bake another 15 minutes, uncovered.

SMALL RED POTATOES ON THE GRILL

Ingredients to serve 6:

12 small, red potatoes (if very small, use 18 or even more)
1 medium onion, peeled, sliced and broken into rings
2 cloves garlic, peeled
4 T fresh herbs of your choosing, such as rosemary or basil (chopped)
3 T olive oil
Parmesan cheese, grated
salt and pepper
2 sheets alumafoil, about 14" x 14"

Rub each of the potatoes with olive oil and place half of them on each of the sheets of the alumafoil.

Place half of the onion rings over the potatoes on each sheet.

Place one clove garlic on each sheet and then sprinkle equal portions of herbs and cheese over the potatoes.

Sprinkle lightly with salt and pepper and generously with Parmesan.

Fold the alumafoil over, making two sealed pockets. Roast over hot coals or 40 minutes.

KAREN'S FAVORITE (herb baked)

Ingredients to serve 6:

6 large potatoes, peeled and diced
1 large onion, peeled and chopped
3 ribs celery, chopped
1 cup green and/or red sweet pepper, chopped
1 T poultry seasoning
1 T chopped fresh parsley
2 T chopped fresh herbs of your choosing (thyme, rosemary, dill, etc.)
3 T olive oil

Combine all ingredients. The oil will help the herbs stick to the vegetables. Spread on a lightly greased cookie sheet and bake in a pre-heated 400 degree oven for 20-30 minutes.

Courtesy Karen Schindler, Phoenix, Arizona.

VEGETABLE MEDLEY ON THE GRILL

Ingredients to serve 4:

4 medium potatoes, cut into bite-size chunks
1 small zucchini, sliced
2 ribs celery, chopped into half-inch pieces
1 cup green beans, cut into 1 inch pieces
1 medium onion, peeled, sliced and broken into rings
3 carrots, sliced
4 T butter or margarine
4 sheets alumafoil, about 12" x 12"
salt and pepper

Place equal portions of all ingredients on the four sheets of foil. Salt and pepper lightly.

Fold sheets into "pockets" and seal with your fingers. Bake over hot coals for about 40 minutes.

Option: Sprinkle with grated cheese of your choosing.

SCALLOPED POTATOES

SCALLOPED POTATOES WITH MUSHROOMS

Ingredients to serve 6-8:

8 large potatoes, sliced thin
2 cups fresh mushrooms, sliced
milk (to cover potatoes)
1 can mushroom soup
4 T. onions, chopped
1 cup mild cheese, grated
salt and pepper
1/8 pound butter

Layer the sliced potatoes in a greased shallow baking dish about 2/3 full. Sauté the onions and mushrooms in butter until tender. Lightly season potatoes. Mix in mushrooms, onions and mushroom soup. Add enough milk to cover all. Bake in medium oven about two hours or until potatoes are tender. Sprinkle cheese on top and return to oven until cheese melts (about 15 minutes). For a meat casserole, add chunks of ham.

SCALLOPED POTATOES WITH PARMESAN

Ingredients to serve 6-8:

6 medium-large potatoes, sliced thin
1 clove garlic, minced
1 small onion, chopped
3 cups chicken broth
Parmesan cheese, grated
parsley, chopped for garnish
salt and pepper

Place sliced potatoes in layers in a lightly greased, flat baking dish or pan.

Sprinkle garlic and onion evenly over potatoes. Pour chicken broth over all.

Season lightly with salt and pepper. Sprinkle generously with Parmesan.

Bake, covered, in a pre-heated 350° oven for 1 hour. Remove cover and bake another 15 minutes.

Sprinkle with chopped parsley before serving.

SCALLOPED POTATOES WITH HAM

Ingredients to serve 8:

8 medium potatoes, peeled and sliced
1-1/2 pounds of ham, diced
1 cn. cream of celery soup
1 cn. cream of onion soup
1-1/2 cups milk
1 cup cheddar cheese, grated or shredded
salt and pepper to taste

Arrange the sliced potatoes in layers in a lightly greased flat baking dish or pan. Use a large enough pan so that there are no more than 2 or 3 layers.
Combine the two cans of soup with the milk and ham. Pour evenly over the potatoes - redistributing some of the ham if necessary.
Sprinkle lightly with salt and pepper.
Sprinkle the cheese evenly, over contents of dish.
Bake covered in a pre-heated 350° oven 1 hour. Take off cover and bake another 15 minutes or until potatoes are tender.

SCALLOPED POTATOES
WITH TOMATOES AND WIENERS

Ingredients to serve 6-8:

8 medium potatoes, peeled and sliced
1 cn. cream of celery soup
1 cn. cream of onion soup
2 cups milk
3 tomatoes, sliced fairly thin
1 pound wieners, sliced
1-1/2 cups Swiss cheese, shredded or grated
salt and pepper to taste

Arrange the sliced potatoes in layers in a lightly greased flat baking dish or pan.
Combine the soups, milk and wiener slices and pour evenly over the potatoes. You may have to rearrange the wiener pieces.
Lightly season with salt and pepper.
Sprinkle the cheese, evenly, over the potatoes.
Bake, covered, one hour in a pre-heated 350° oven. Uncover and bake another 15 minutes or until potatoes are tender.
Arrange tomato slices over the contents.

Section IV
SKILLET POTATOES

MINNESOTA SKILLET BREAKFAST

Ingredients to serve 4:

6 medium red potatoes cut into chunks

8 eggs, beaten

1 pound pork sausage (bulk type)

1 medium onion, peeled and chopped

1 cup cheddar cheese, grated or shredded

2 T vegetable oil

salt and pepper to taste

Cook the potato chunks in water in a covered sauce pan for about 20 minutes or until soft.

Meanwhile, brown the crumbled sausage and chopped onion in vegetable oil on top of the stove but in an oven proof skillet.

When the potatoes are done, add them and the beaten eggs to the skillet. Season lightly with salt and pepper and then stir all ingredients together in the pan.

Cook over medium plus heat, stirring regularly, until eggs are cooked.

Sprinkle cheese on top and place under a broiler a couple of minutes or until cheese is melted.

Serve in pie shaped pieces. (cut with a knife and remove from the skillet with a spatula)

NORTH DAKOTA SKILLET BREAKFAST

Ingredients to serve 4:

1 pkg. frozen hashbrowns, thawed

8 eggs

1-1/2 cups pre-cooked ham, diced

1 medium onion, peeled and chopped

salt and pepper to taste

1-1/2 cups shredded or grated cheese of your choosing

3 T vegetable oil

Sauté the onion, ham and hashbrowns in oil in a skillet; stirring regularly for about 10 minutes over medium heat.

Beat the eggs. Stir in about 1/2 t pepper and 1/4 t salt. Stir eggs into the contents of the skillet and continue cooking until eggs solidify.

Sprinkle cheese over skillet contents and place briefly under a broiler until the cheese melts. Watch carefully; it should only take a minute or two.

Cut with a knife and use a spatula to remove the four, pie-shaped pieces.

HASHBROWNS FROM LEFT-OVER BAKED OR BOILED POTATOES

Ingredients to serve 4:

4 cups diced left-over baked or boiled potatoes

4 T chopped onion

3 T vegetable oil

1 T minced herbs of your choosing (rosemary, thyme, basil, etc.)

1/2 t salt

1/4 t pepper

3 T butter

Sauté the chopped onion in the oil in a skillet a couple of minutes or until onion is clear.

Remove onion with a slotted spoon and combine in a bowl with the potatoes and seasonings.

Discard oil remaining in a skillet. Replace with butter. As soon as butter has melted, pour all contents of the bowl into the skillet. Fry over medium plus heat until the hashbrowns take on a golden color. Toss occasionally or they may burn.

POTATO OMELET

Ingredients to serve 4:

8 eggs

4 medium potatoes, peeled and chopped

1 medium onion, peeled and chopped

2 cloves garlic, peeled and minced

1/2 cup water

8 slices bacon fried crisp and crumbled

4 T oil

salt and pepper to taste

Fry the chopped potatoes, onion and garlic in a skillet in oil over medium heat.

Whisk the eggs in the water and when the potatoes are soft (about 10 minutes) pour the egg mixture over the contents of the skillet. Continue to cook about 7 or 8 minutes or until the eggs are well set. Sprinkle the bacon bits over-all, then cut with a knife and serve with a spatula.

POTATO SAUSAGE DINNER IN A FRYING PAN

Ingredients to serve 4:

1 pound ground sausage or sausage in casings, cooked
4 large potatoes, boiled and sliced
1 medium onion, chopped
3 T green pepper, chopped
3 T butter
salt and pepper to taste

Boil the sausages or fry the ground sausage.

Boil the potatoes (leave skins on if they are new potatoes) until they are easily penetrated with a fork, but do not over-cook. Slice the potatoes.

If sausage in casings is used, slice about 1/3 inch thick. Almost any kind of sausage works well; it just depends on your taste whether you want a spicy or a mild dish.

Melt the butter in an iron skillet, add all ingredients and stir together. Stir occasionally (over medium heat) so as not to burn.

Serve when all ingredients are piping hot.

POTATOES O'BRIEN FROM LEFT-OVERS

Ingredients to serve 4:

4 cups diced, left-over baked or boiled potatoes
4 T chopped onion
4 T chopped green pepper
4 T chopped red pepper or pimento
1 t minced garlic
4 T melted butter
salt and pepper to taste

Sauté the onion, garlic and peppers in the butter a couple of minutes or until the onion is clear.

If there is not enough melted butter left to cover the bottom of the skillet, add more butter. Add the diced potatoes and stir together until well mixed.

Cook over medium plus heat until potatoes turn golden in color.

ZESTY RAW FRIES

Ingredients to serve 6:

6 medium potatoes, sliced (leave skins on if in good condition)
4 T vegetable oil
1 small onion, peeled and chopped
1 t minced garlic
1 T chopped fresh herbs, such as oregano, thyme, basil or rosemary
1 t dry Italian dressing
salt and pepper to taste

Cover the bottom of a skillet with the cooking oil. Combine all ingredients in the pan and fry over medium plus heat, stirring occasionally to prevent burning.
Potatoes should be done in about 15 minutes.

SEASONED RAW FRIES WITH CHEESE

Ingredients to serve 6:

6 medium to large potatoes, sliced
4 T vegetable oil
1 T chopped fresh herbs (thyme, rosemary, basil etc.)
1 T dry mustard
1/2 t pepper
1-1/2 cups grated cheese of your choosing (cheddar, Swiss, Monterey Jack, etc.)

Fry the sliced potatoes in the oil in an oven proof skillet. Sprinkle the seasonings over the potatoes. Fry over medium plus heat, turning regularly to prevent burning. Fries should be done in 10 to 15 minutes. Remove from heat, sprinkle with cheese. Place in a pre-heated oven or under a broiler until cheese melts. Watch carefully so cheese does not burn.

FRIED WHOLE POTATOES

Ingredients to serve 4:

20 to 30 very small new potatoes; adjust number accordingly to size
4 T olive oil
1 T chopped fresh thyme
1 T chopped fresh rosemary
1 T chopped parsley
salt and pepper

Fry the potatoes in olive oil in a skillet over medium plus heat.

Sprinkle with herbs and seasonings but go easy on the salt and pepper. Roll the potatoes from time to time while they are frying so that the seasonings will be on all sides and the potatoes will be uniformly cooked.

Potatoes should be done in about 15 minutes but test occasionally with a fork.

ZESTY POTATO WEDGES

Ingredients to serve 6:

6 medium to large potatoes, peeled and cut into wedges
1 medium onion, peeled and chopped
6 bacon strips, cut into half-inch pieces
1/4 cup cider vinegar
1 t chopped oregano
1 t chopped thyme
1 clove garlic, minced
1 t chopped rosemary
1/4 t pepper
1/2 t salt

Boil the potato wedges in water in a covered sauce pan about 10 minutes or until they just start to soften.

Meanwhile, fry the bacon pieces over medium heat until crisp. Remove bacon with a slotted spoon.

Sauté the onion and garlic in a skillet in the bacon grease a couple of minutes or until the onion is clear.

Add the partially cooked potatoes to the skillet and sprinkle with seasonings. Fry another 10 minutes or until potatoes are done, turning occasionally to coat the potatoes with the seasonings.

Serve in a bowl. Sprinkle with the bacon bits just before serving.

POTATOES WITH CABBAGE

Ingredients to serve 6:

4 large potatoes, quartered
1 medium head of cabbage - about the equivalent of the potatoes, cut into bite-size chunks
4 T olive oil
1 t garlic salt
1/2 t pepper
1/4 pound butter, cut into pats

Cover the potatoes with water and cook in a covered sauce pan about 10 minutes.

Meanwhile, core the cabbage and cut remainder into bite-size chunks. Add to the kettle after the potatoes have been cooking for 10 minutes. Add hot water to cover if necessary. Cook another 10 minutes, covered or until vegetables are soft.

Cover the bottom of a large skillet with the olive oil. Add the potatoes, cabbage and seasonings. Fry over medium heat for about 5 minutes, turning occasionally. Remove from heat. With a large spoon or potato masher, mash the vegetables and work them together.

Return to heat a few minutes, turning with a spatula until both sides start to brown.

Serve with pats of butter.

REALLY "SCALLOPED" POTATOES

Ingredients to serve 4:

6 medium potatoes, peeled and sliced fairly thin

4 T olive oil, divided

1 pound fresh scallops

2 T chopped, fresh dill

1 small onion, peeled and chopped

2 cloves garlic, peeled and minced

salt and pepper to taste

Using half the oil, fry the sliced potatoes, onion and garlic over medium heat. When the potatoes are soft (10-12 minutes), remove the potatoes, onions, and garlic with a slotted spoon. Add the remainder of the oil to the skillet.

Sauté the scallops in the oil over medium heat for 3 or 4 minutes or until opaque.

Combine the scallops with the potatoes, onion and garlic in a serving bowl.

Garnish with chopped dill.

GLAZED POTATOES

Ingredients to serve 4:

8 small to medium potatoes

1/2 cup sugar

1/2 stick butter or margarine

Using a covered sauce pan, boil the potatoes about 20 minutes or until done—test with a fork. Drain and let cool to handle, then peel.

Sprinkle sugar over the bottom of a skillet (preferably non-stick). Heat until sugar melts but is still clear. Add the butter; when it melts, add the potatoes. Roll the potatoes around until they are well covered and thoroughly heated.

FRIED POTATOES WITH BACON BITS

Ingredients to serve 4:

6 medium potatoes, sliced, with or without skins on and pre-cooked
6 slices bacon, cut the short way into narrow (1/2 inch) strips
1 medium onion, chopped

Fry the bacon bits in a skillet until grease starts to form. Add the onions and sauté until they become translucent. Pour off excess grease. Add the pre-cooked, sliced potatoes. Add pepper to taste.

LOGGING CAMP HASHBROWNS

Ingredients to serve 8-10:

40 oz. (13 1/2 c) frozen shredded hashbrowns
1/3 c onion chopped
2 c shredded cheese (mixture of Cheddar and Monterey Jack cheeses)
1/2 tsp. black pepper
1/2 tsp. salt
1 can cream of chicken soup
1/2 c (1 stick) margarine, melted

Preheat oven to 450° degrees. In large mixing bowl, combine the hashbrowns, onions, shredded cheese, pepper and salt. Add cream of chicken soup; mix thoroughly. Add melted margarine, mix.
Grease a 9 by 13-inch pan with additional margarine. Transfer mixture into greased pan and spread out evenly. Do no pack down. Bake for 1 hour on top rack of oven or until golden brown. Rotate pan for even browning if necessary. Let stand 5 minutes before serving.

Courtesy Dr. and Mrs. Peter Brenny, Staples, Minnesota.

HASH

HASH WITH PORK SAUSAGE

Ingredients to serve 6:

6 potatoes, diced small
1 pound bulk pork sausage
1 medium onion, peeled and chopped
2 medium carrots, sliced thin
4 T chopped green pepper (or red)
salt and pepper to taste
2 T oil
8 eggs, poached

Cook the diced potatoes in water in a covered sauce pan for about 20 minutes or until potatoes are tender.

Meanwhile, brown the crumbled sausage, onion, carrots and green pepper in the oil in a skillet over medium heat.

Drain the potatoes and add them to the skillet. Stir everything together and fry another 5 minutes.

Meanwhile, poach the eggs. Serve them over the hash.

HASH WITH A MEXICAN TOUCH

Ingredients to serve 4:

8 eggs poached or fried
4 large potatoes, peeled and diced, small
8 bacon strips
1 small onion, peeled and chopped
1 t minced garlic
1 cn. (4 oz.) chopped green chilis
1/2 cup salsa

Cook the diced potatoes in a covered sauce pan for about 20 minutes or until soft.

Meanwhile, fry the bacon in a skillet. Remove when crisp. Save 2 T bacon grease in the skillet.

Sauté the onion, garlic and chilis a couple of minutes or until the onion is clear.

Drain the potatoes and add them and the salsa to the pan; continue cooking for another 5 minutes.

Meanwhile, poach or fry the eggs as requested.

Serve the eggs on the hash.

Option: serve with additional salsa.

HASH WITH POULTRY

Ingredients to serve 6:

6 medium to large potatoes, peeled and diced fine
2 cups diced left-over chicken, turkey, pheasant - whatever!
1 medium onion, peeled and chopped
3 T chopped green pepper
3 T vegetable oil
1/2 t salt
1/4 t pepper
1 t poultry seasoning
6-12 eggs, poached or fried to order

Cover the diced potatoes with water (in a sauce pan) and cook, covered, for 20 minutes or until soft. Drain.

Sauté the onion in a skillet in the oil a couple of minutes until onion is clear.

Add all ingredients (except the eggs) to the skillet. Cook over medium heat for about 20 minutes, stirring regularly. Do not let burn.

Serve with eggs - prepared to order.

CORNED BEEF HASH

Ingredients to serve 6:

6 medium to large potatoes, peeled and diced
2 cups corned beef, diced (left-over beef roast may be substituted)
1 medium onion, peeled and chopped
2 T cooking oil
1 T catsup
3 T chopped green pepper
1/2 t salt
1/4 t pepper
6-12 eggs

If beef is substituted, add 2 T Worcestershire sauce.

Cook the diced potatoes in water in a covered sauce pan for 20 minutes or until potatoes are soft.

Sauté the chopped onion in a skillet in the oil a couple of minutes or until the onion is clear.

Drain the potatoes. Add potatoes and all other ingredients to the skillet. Cook over medium heat about 20 minutes, turning occasionally with a spatula. Brown but do not let burn.

Prepare eggs as requested; serve over hash.

Section V
MASHED POTATOES

Although any variety of potato can be mashed, some work better than others. Based on my experience, I would rank russets best and reds poorest, with everything else somewhere in between. Yukon Gold would also rank close to the top.

From the nutritionist's point of view, potatoes should be boiled whole with skins on, cooled, and then peeled. But this takes considerably longer. If time is a concern then peel and quarter (smaller pieces for large potatoes) them first. To prevent discoloration, keep the potato chunks in cold water until you are ready to cook them.

Cover the quartered potatoes with about an inch of water above the potatoes and let them boil about 20 minutes in a covered sauce pan. Test them occasionally with a fork; they should slip off the fork. You want them done but not mushy.

Drain the cooked potatoes and then return them to the stove for a couple of minutes to dry them.

Milk and butter are traditional additives. For enough potatoes to serve 4 (four large potatoes) heat 1/2 cup of milk and 4 T butter together until the butter melts. Do not let boil.

All of the following recipes for mashed potatoes may be "riced".

Combine the potatoes, milk and butter with a potato masher or electric mixer; do not use a food processor.

In addition to milk and butter there are many other possibilities for additives. For enough potatoes to *serve 4*, try any of the following – or combinations thereof:

> 4 strips bacon, fried and crumbled
>
> 4 T cheese of your choosing, grated or shredded
>
> 1/2 cup French fried onions (come in a can)
>
> 3 T chopped chives
>
> 3 T chopped green onions (either or both white and green parts)
>
> 3 T chopped sweet or mild onions,
>
> 1 2 oz. jar chopped pimentos,
>
> 2 T processed horseradish
>
> 3 T creamed horseradish

3 cloves garlic, peeled, sautéed and minced
2 T chopped fresh herbs of your choosing, (basil, dill, thyme, etc.)
2 T chopped pitted olives (black, green or stuffed)
1 medium turnip, cooked and mashed
1 medium rutabaga, cooked and mashed
1 medium sweet potato, cooked and mashed
4 T fried and crumbled pork sausage
3 T chopped summer sausage or other luncheon meat

*Consult Baked Potato Section for more baked mashed potato recipes

MASHED POTATOES WITH A COMBINATION OF ADDITIVES

Ingredients to serve 6:
6 large potatoes, peeled and cut into chunks
1/2 stick butter or margarine, melted
2 cloves garlic, minced
1 small onion, peeled and minced
1 rib celery, chopped
6 slices bacon, fried and crumbled
3 T cheddar cheese, grated or shredded
2/3 cup milk
salt to taste

Peel and cut the potatoes into chunks. Boil in water in a covered sauce pan for 20 minutes or until they will slide off a fork.

Meanwhile, fry the bacon, let cool and crumble.

While the potatoes are cooking, sauté the onion, celery, and garlic in the butter in a skillet. (You may use the same skillet you fried the bacon in, but pour off the bacon grease.)

When the potatoes are done, drain them and then return to the stove for a couple of minutes to dry them.

Mash together all ingredients, including the butter used to sauté the vegetables. Use a potato masher or an electric mixer. Do not use a food processor.

ANOTHER WAY TO FLAVOR MASHED POTATOES

Ingredients to serve 4:
4 large potatoes, peeled and chunked
6 whole peppercorns
1 bay leaf
1/2 t garlic salt
1/2 cup milk
1/3 stick butter, melted

Cover the potatoes with water in a sauce pan. Add the peppercorns, bay leaf and garlic salt to the water. Boil, covered, for 20 minutes or until the potatoes are done – test with a fork.

Remove the bay leaf and peppercorns with a slotted spoon and discard. Drain the potatoes; return to the stove for a couple of minutes to dry the potatoes.

Combine all remaining ingredients and mash with a hand masher or electric mixer.

MASHED BAKED POTATOES

Ingredients to serve 6:

6 large potatoes
1/2 stick butter or margarine, melted
1/2 cup milk, warmed
1/2 t salt
1/4 t pepper

Bake the potatoes in a pre-heated 375° oven for 1 hour (middle shelf) or until done. Test with a fork.

Remove the potatoes from the oven and let cool enough to handle.

Cut the potatoes in two—lengthwise and scoop out "meat". Place in a large bowl. Mash with a fork.

Add all other ingredients and mash with a hand masher or electric mixer.

Re-heat the potatoes; do not let burn.

You will find these mashed potatoes will have a different but delightful flavor.

MASHED POTATOES WITH DILL

Ingredients to serve 4:

4 large potatoes, peeled and chunked
1/2 stick butter or margarine, melted
3 T chopped fresh dill
1/2 cup milk
1/2 t salt
1/4 t pepper

Place the chunked potatoes in a sauce pan and cover with water (about 1 inch over the tops of the potatoes). Boil, covered, about 20 minutes or until done—test with a fork. Drain and return to the stove a couple of minutes to dry.

Mash together all ingredients; use a hand masher or an electric mixer (never a food processor).

MASHED POTATOES WITH GARLIC AND ONION

Ingredients to serve 6:

6 large potatoes, peeled and chunked
4 cloves garlic, peeled and minced
1 small onion, peeled and minced
1/2 stick butter or margarine
1/2 cup milk (or sour cream or buttermilk)
1/2 t salt
1/4 t pepper

Cover the potato chunks with water in a sauce pan. Boil (covered) about 20 minutes or until done (test with a fork).

Meanwhile, sauté the minced onion and garlic in the butter.

Mash together all ingredients, including the butter used to sauté the onion and garlic. Use a hand masher or electric mixer.

ROOT-MOOS (RUTABAGAS AND POTATOES)
A SWEDISH RECIPE

Use equal portions (by volume) of rutabagas and potatoes.

Cover with water, add a dash of salt and boil together until soft enough to mash. Remove from the water and mash them together. Add a pat of butter and a little milk from time to time and mash and stir until thoroughly blended.

Add salt and pepper to taste.

Serve as a vegetable with the meal.

MASHED POTATOES WITH MUSHROOMS

Ingredients to serve 4:

4 large potatoes, peeled and chunked
1 cn. cream of mushroom soup
1/2 cup fresh mushrooms, chopped or a 2 oz. cn. of mushrooms
1/2 cup milk
1 small onion, chopped
1/2 stick butter or margarine, melted
1/2 t salt
1/4 t pepper

In a sauce pan, cover the potatoes with water and boil — covered — for about 20 minutes or until done — test with a fork.

Meanwhile, sauté the chopped onion in the melted butter for a couple of minutes or until onion is clear.

Drain the potatoes and return to the stove a couple of minutes to dry.

Using a hand masher or electric mixer, combine all ingredients including the butter used to sauté the onion.

CREAMY MASHED POTATOES

Ingredients to serve 6:

6 large potatoes, peeled and chunked
3/4 cup heavy cream
1/2 stick butter or margarine, melted
4 T chopped chives or green onion (both white and green parts)
1 T chopped fresh thyme
1/2 t salt
1/4 t pepper

Boil the chunked potatoes in water in a covered sauce pan for 20 minutes or until done, check with a fork.
Drain and then return to the stove a couple of minutes to dry the potatoes.
Mash together all ingredients. Use a hand masher or electric mixer.

MASHED POTATOES WITH BROWNED ONIONS

Ingredients to serve 4:

4 large potatoes, peeled and chunked
1 medium onion, peeled, sliced and broken into rings
1/2 cup milk
1/2 cup sour cream
1/2 stick butter or margarine, melted
1/2 t salt
1/2 t pepper

Boil the potato chunks for about 20 minutes in a covered sauce pan - check with a fork. Drain and return to the stove a couple of minutes to dry.
Meanwhile, sauté the broken onion rings in the butter. Let cook until the onions turn brown (but do not burn).
Mash together all ingredients, including the butter used to sauté the onion. Use a hand masher or electric mixer.
A half-can of French fried onions may be substituted for the fresh onion.

MASHED POTATOES ON BRATS

Ingredients to serve 4:

8 brats or wieners, sliced length-wise
2 large potatoes, peeled and chunked
8 T grated or shredded cheese (cheddar works well)
1/2 cup milk
2 T butter or margarine, melted
salt and pepper to taste

Boil the chunked potatoes in water in a covered sauce pan for about 20 minutes or until done. (check with a fork) Drain and return to the stove for a couple of minutes to dry the potatoes.

Slice the brats or wieners length-wise but leave the halves attached with a little skin.

Mash the potatoes, milk and butter together.

Spoon the mashed potatoes on top of the brats or wieners. Season lightly with salt and pepper. Sprinkle with the cheese.

Bake in a pre-heated 375° oven for about 15 minutes or until the cheese melts.

MASHED POTATOES WITH BLUE CHEESE

Ingredients to serve 4:

4 large potatoes, peeled and chunked

1/3 cup blue cheese, crumbled

1/3 cup milk

1 small onion, peeled and chopped

1/2 stick butter or margarine, melted

1/2 t salt

1/4 t pepper

Boil the potatoes in a sauce pan, covered, for about 20 minutes or until done – check with a fork. Drain and return to the stove a couple of minutes to dry the potatoes.

Mash together all ingredients; use a hand masher or electric mixer.

If you really like blue cheese, try a little more than 1/3 cup.

MASHED POTATOES WITH CREAM CHEESE

Ingredients to serve 6:

6 large potatoes, peeled and chunked

1 3 oz. pkg. cream cheese, softened

1/2 cup sour cream

1/2 stick butter or margarine, melted

3 T chopped chives

1/2 t salt

1/4 t pepper

Boil the potato chunks in water in a covered sauce pan for 20 minutes or until done - test with a fork. Drain and return to the stove for a couple of minutes to dry the potatoes.

Mash together all ingredients. Use a hand masher or electric mixer.

If you really like cream cheese, try a little more than the 3 oz. called for.

MASHED POTATOES WITH CHICKEN BROTH

Ingredients to serve 6:

6 large potatoes, peeled and chunked
2 cns. chicken broth, divided
1/2 stick butter or margarine, melted
1/4 t pepper

Boil the chunked potatoes in 1 cup chicken broth and as much water as needed to cover the potatoes. Use a covered sauce pan and cook for 20 minutes or until done. Check with a fork. Drain and return to the stove for a couple of minutes to dry the potatoes.

Mash together all the ingredients, including the reserved cup of chicken broth. Use a hand masher or electric mixer. Do not add salt

MASHED POTATOES WITH SWEET POTATOES

Ingredients to serve 4:

3 large potatoes
1 large sweet potato
1/2 stick butter or margarine, melted
1/2 cup half and half
1/2 t salt
1/4 t pepper
1 T brown sugar

Cover all four potatoes with water (skins on) and boil for 25 minutes or until done - check with a fork. Let cool and peel. Cut into chunks.

Mash together all ingredients. Use a hand masher or electric mixer. Re-heat.

MASHED POTATOES WITH A TOUCH OF MUSTARD

Ingredients to serve 4:

4 large potatoes, peeled and quartered
1/2 cup milk
1/2 stick butter or margarine, melted
3 t dry mustard
1/2 t salt
1/4 t pepper

Cover the potato chunks with water and boil (covered) for about 20 minutes or until done - check with a fork. Drain and return to the stove a couple of minutes to dry the potatoes.

Mash together all ingredients. Try to distribute the mustard evenly. If you cannot taste the mustard, add a little more. Use a hand masher or electric mixer.

MASHED POTATOES WITH SWEET PEPPERS

Ingredients to serve 6:

6 large potatoes, peeled and chunked
1/3 cup finely chopped sweet red bell pepper
1/3 cup finely chopped sweet green bell pepper
1 cup milk
1 cup sour cream
3 T butter, melted
2 T creamed horseradish
3 green onions, chopped, white parts only
1/2 t salt
1/4 t pepper

Cover the chunked potatoes with water and boil in a covered sauce pan for 20 minutes or until done - check with a fork. Drain and return to the stove to dry potatoes.

Mash together all ingredients. Use a hand masher or electric mixer.

MASHED POTATOES WITH ARTICHOKE HEARTS

Ingredients to serve 6:

6 large potatoes, peeled and chunked
1 cn. artichoke hearts (16 oz.)
1/2 stick butter or margarine, melted
1/2 cup milk, heated
1/2 t salt
1/4 t pepper

In a sauce pan, cover the potatoes with water and boil (covered) about 20 minutes or until done – test with a fork.

Meanwhile, drain the can of artichoke hearts. Add the milk to the hearts and purée until fairly smooth.

Drain the potatoes and return to the stove for a couple of minutes to dry the potatoes.

Combine all ingredients and mash or use an electric mixer. You may need to re-heat.

CHEESY MASHED POTATOES

Ingredients to serve 6:

6 large potatoes, peeled and chunked
1 cup cheddar cheese, grated or shredded
1 cup Monterey Jack cheese, grated or shredded
1/2 stick butter or margarine, melted
1/2 cup milk, warmed
1/2 cup chopped chives
1/2 t salt
1/4 t pepper

In a sauce pan, cover the potatoes with water and boil covered, about 20 minutes or until done — test with a fork. Drain and return to the stove for a couple of minutes to dry the potatoes.

Combine all ingredients with a hand masher or electric mixer.

Because of the relatively large amount of cheese, you may need to reheat the potatoes a little.

HALLOWEEN MASHED POTATOES

Ingredients to serve 6:

6 large potatoes, peeled and chunked

1 large pumpkin, seeds and fiber removed

1 cn. pumpkin

1/2 cup milk, warmed

1/2 stick butter or margarine, melted

1/2 t nutmeg

1/2 t salt

1/4 t pepper

Slice off the top 1/4 of the pumpkin, save. Remove the seeds and fiber. Bake in a pre-heated 375° oven 45 minutes or until the meat starts to soften.

During the last half-hour, cover the potatoes with water in a sauce pan and boil for 20 minutes or until done - test with a fork. Drain and return to the stove for a couple of minutes to dry the potatoes.

Mash together the potatoes, canned pumpkin, melted butter, milk and seasonings.

Remove the pumpkin from the oven with hot pads and place on a platter. Spoon the mashed potatoes into the pumpkin; replace the top and serve.

MASHED POTATOES WITH GARDEN PEAS AND BACON

Ingredients to serve 4:

4 large potatoes, peeled and quartered

1/2 pound bacon, fried and crumbled

3 T chopped onion

1-1/2 cups fresh garden peas

1/2 stick butter or margarine, melted

1/2 cup milk, warmed

1/2 t salt

1/4 t pepper

In a sauce pan, cover the potatoes with water and boil, covered, about 20 minutes or until done - test with a fork.

Drain and return to the stove for a couple of minutes to dry the potatoes.

Meanwhile, fry and crumble the bacon.

Also while the potatoes are cooking, sauté the onion in a little of the butter (or use bacon grease).

Combine all ingredients and mash with a hand masher or electric mixer.

GARLIC POTATOES

Ingredients to serve 4:

4 large potatoes, peeled and chunked
4 cloves garlic, peeled (depends on how much you like garlic)
1/2 stick butter or margarine, melted
1/2 cup milk, warmed
1/4 t pepper

In a sauce pan, cover the potatoes with water and boil, covered for about 20 minuets or until done - test with a fork.

Meanwhile, in a separate sauce pan, cover the peeled garlic cloves with water and boil 5 minutes. Drain and let cool. When cool enough to handle safely, mince the garlic.

Combine all ingredients and mash with a hand masher or electric mixer.

MICROWAVE MASHED POTATOES

Ingredients to serve 6:

6 large potatoes, peeled and chunked
1 medium onion, peeled and broken into rings
1/2 stick butter or margarine, melted
1 rib celery, chopped
2 cloves garlic, peeled and minced
1/2 t salt
1/4 t pepper
parsley for garnish

Using a micro-safe casserole dish, combine all ingredients thoroughly. Cook at full power for 5 minutes. Stir thoroughly. Cook on high another 5 minutes. Check to be sure potatoes are done before serving. Garnish with parsley flakes or 3 T chopped, fresh parsley. Chopped chives may be substituted.

WARMED UP MASHED POTATOES

To make leftover mashed potatoes like new, warm them up the next day in a double boiler. You will need to add a little milk and perhaps some melted butter.

Section VI
POTATO CASSEROLES

CREAMY CASSEROLE OF HASH BROWNS

Ingredients to serve 6-8:

1 32 oz. pkg. frozen hashbrowns, thawed
2 cups cheddar cheese, grated or shredded
1 cup diced ham or bacon bits
1 cn. cream of chicken soup
2 cups sour cream
1 stick butter or margarine, melted and divided
1 small onion, peeled, sliced and broken into rings
seasoned bread crumbs

Combine all ingredients except half the butter and the bread crumbs in an oven-proof casserole dish.
Drizzle the remainder of the butter over the mixture.
Sprinkle generously with seasoned bread crumbs.
Bake in a pre-heated 350° oven on the middle shelf one hour. If the crumbs start to burn, lower the heat and bake a little longer.

CRUSTY POTATO CASSEROLE SQUARES

Ingredients to serve 6-8:

5 large baking potatoes, peeled and shredded (approximately 8 cups) cover with water to keep white
1/4 cup butter
1 cup milk
1 cup water from the drained potatoes
2 small or one large onion, peeled and chopped
1-1/2 t salt
1/2 t pepper
4 lightly beaten eggs
paprika

Drain the potatoes. Keep 1 cup of water to heat with the butter and the milk to just under boiling. Pour over the potatoes and stir in the salt, pepper and eggs.

Melt another 2 T butter to coat the bottom and sides of a 9"x13" casserole. Pour in the potato mixture. Sprinkle with paprika.

Bake uncovered at 375° degrees until set in the center and lightly browned (about 50 minutes.)

Makes 10 to 12 squares (cut with knife and remove with spatula)

Courtesy Karen Cowie, Gull Lake, Brainerd, Minnesota.

POTATO-HALIBUT CASSEROLE

Ingredients to serve 4:

3 large potatoes, peeled and sliced
3 cups halibut, flaked
2 hard-boiled eggs, sliced
1/2 stick butter or margarine, melted and divided
2 cups milk
4 T flour
1/2 t salt
1/4 t pepper
bread crumbs

Place the eggs in cold water, bring to a boil; let sit 10 minutes; remove from water and let cool. Peel and slice.

Prepare a white sauce from 1/2 of the melted butter, milk, flour and salt. Heat and stir until it starts to thicken.

Using a lightly greased baking dish or pan (about 12 x 12), layer half the potatoes and then half the halibut on the bottom. Next add a layer of sliced eggs. Pour half the white sauce over this. Layer the rest of the potatoes and the halibut on top. Pour the remainder of the white sauce over this.

Sprinkle, generously, with seasoned bread crumbs and drizzle the rest of the butter over-all.

Bake 30 minutes in a pre-heated, 400° oven, uncovered; use the middle shelf. If the crumbs start to burn, reduce heat and bake longer or place on a lower shelf. Check potatoes for doneness before serving.

POTATO-WALLEYE CASSEROLE

Ingredients to serve 4:

4 walleye fillets, about 8 oz. each
4 large potatoes, peeled and sliced – about 1/2 inch thick
1 small onion, peeled, sliced and broken into rings
1 cup milk
2 T minced, fresh dill
Parmesan cheese, grated
1/2 t salt
1/4 t pepper
lemon pepper

In a sauce pan, cover the potato slices with water and boil (covered) 15 minutes or until they just start to soften. Drain and cool to handle.

Using a lightly greased 12 x 12 baking dish or pan, layer the potato slices on the bottom. Pour the milk over the potatoes. Layer the onion rings on top of the potatoes. Lightly season with salt and pepper.

Lay the 4 fish fillets on top of the onion rings, side by side. Season with lemon pepper. Sprinkle with chopped dill. Sprinkle with Parmesan cheese (about 1 T per fillet.

Bake, uncovered, in a 350° oven 20 minutes or until the fish flake easily with a fork.

MASHED POTATO CASSEROLE

Ingredients to serve 6:

3 cups mashed potatoes, including 1/2 cup milk blended in

3 eggs, separated

1/2 cup sour cream

1 3 oz. pkg. cream cheese, softened

1/2 stick butter or margarine, melted and divided

1/2 t salt

1/4 t pepper

2 T minced fresh herbs (thyme, oregano or your favorite)

Combine the potatoes, cheese, egg yolks, sour cream and half the butter.

Beat the egg whites until they start to "peak". Stir the egg whites into the potato mixture.

Spoon potatoes into a lightly greased baking dish or pan. Sprinkle herbs on top. Season lightly with salt and pepper. Drizzle the remaining butter over-all. Bake, uncovered, in 350°, pre-heated oven for 1 hour.

POTATO, PEAS AND EGGS CASSEROLE

Ingredients to serve 5-6:

4 large potatoes, peeled and sliced about 1/2 inch thick

6 eggs, hard-boiled and sliced

2 cns. peas, drained or 2 cups fresh, garden peas

1 small onion, peeled, sliced and broken into rings

1/2 stick butter or margarine, melted and divided

2 cups milk

1/2 t salt

1/4 t pepper

1-1/2 cups corn flakes, crushed fine

In a sauce pan, cover the potato slices with water and boil (covered) for about 15 minutes or until the potatoes start to soften. Drain and cool.

Meanwhile, in a sauce pan, cover the eggs with water, bring to a boil; remove from heat; let stand 10 minutes. Let cool to handle, peel and slice - thin.

Using a lightly greased oven-proof casserole dish or pan, place one layer of the partially cooked potatoes on the bottom. Sprinkle a layer of peas over the potatoes. Arrange the onion slices on top of the peas. Add a layer of sliced eggs (about half of them). Continue layering potatoes, eggs and onions.

Pour the milk over all - it should come up about 2/3 of the way on the ingredients.

Season lightly with salt and pepper. Cover with the crushed corn flakes.

Bake in a pre-heated 350° oven for 1 hour or until the potatoes are soft.

HASH BROWNS IN A CROCK POT #1

Ingredients to serve 6:

1 32 oz. pkg. frozen hash browns, thawed
1 cup shredded or grated cheese of your choice
1 cn. cream of celery soup
1 cup sour cream
1-1/2 cups diced ham

Combine all ingredients in a crock pot. Cook on high, covered, 2 hours and 2 hours on low.

HASH BROWNS IN A CROCK POT #2

Ingredients to serve 6:

1 32 oz. pkg. frozen O'Brien style hash browns, thawed
2 cns. cheddar cheese soup
2 cups cheddar cheese, shredded or grated
1 cup half and half

Combine all ingredients in a crock pot. Cook on high (covered) 2 hours and on low another 2 hours or until potatoes are done.

POTATO-SPINACH CASSEROLE

Ingredients to serve 6:

4 large potatoes, peeled and chunked
1 pkg. (10 oz.) frozen spinach, thawed
3 eggs, beaten
1/2 stick butter or margarine, divided

1 cup half and half
2 cups cheddar cheese, grated or shredded, divided
1/2 t salt
1/4 t pepper

In a sauce pan, cover the potato chunks with water and boil (covered) for about 20 minutes or until potatoes are done - test with a fork. Drain and then return to the stove for a couple of minutes to dry the potatoes.

Combine half the cheese, half the melted butter, the half and half, beaten eggs, salt and pepper. Mash together with a hand masher or electric mixer.

Cover the bottom of a skillet with water; bring to a boil; add the spinach and toss for only 1 minute or until the spinach starts to wilt.

Spoon about half of the potato mixture evenly across the bottom of a lightly greased baking dish or pan. Layer the spinach over the potatoes, evenly. Cover with the balance of the potato mixture.

Sprinkle the rest of the cheese and melted butter over all and bake in a pre-heated 375° oven until the cheese melts.

POTATO CASSEROLE WITH A MEXICAN TOUCH

Ingredients to serve 6:

1 32 oz. pkg. frozen hash browns - O'Brien style, thawed
2 cups diced ham
3 eggs, beaten
1-1/2 cups milk
1 small onion, peeled and chopped
1-1/2 cups Monterey Jack cheese, grated or shredded
1 4 oz. cn. Jalapeno peppers, chopped (use kitchen gloves)

Combine all ingredients except the milk and eggs.
Spoon the potato mixture into a lightly greased baking dish or pan.
Beat the eggs into the milk (lightly). Pour the milk-egg mixture over the potatoes.
Bake in a pre-heated 375° oven for 45 minutes (uncovered).

POTATO WITH CRAB MEAT CASSEROLE

Ingredients to serve 4:

4 large potatoes, peeled and sliced
1-1/2 cups cream
1/2 stick butter, melted
1 pound crab meat (could use scallops or other seafood)
salt and pepper
Parmesan, grated

Arrange one layer of sliced potatoes in a lightly greased casserole or other oven-proof dish. Arrange a layer of crab meat on the potatoes, then another layer of potatoes and another layer of crab meat until those ingredients are used up.

Sprinkle each layer lightly with salt and pepper as you go.

Pour the cream and melted butter over-all.

Sprinkle generously with grated Parmesan cheese.

Bake, 1 hour, covered, in a pre-heated 375° oven. Remove cover and continue baking about 30 minutes or until potatoes are soft.

BRITISH SHEPHERD'S PIE

Ingredients to serve 6:

6 large potatoes, peeled and chunked

1-1/2 pounds ground beef or chopped steak

1/2 stick butter or margarine, melted and divided

1/2 cup milk

1 t salt, divided

1/2 t pepper, divided

1 large onion, peeled, sliced and divided into rings

2 carrots, peeled and sliced thin

2 ribs celery, chopped

2 cups beef broth

1 cup peas

3 T flour

Cover potatoes with water in a sauce pan and boil, covered, 20 minutes or until done - test with a fork. Add the milk, 1/2 t salt, 1/4 t pepper and 1/2 of the melted butter and mash with a hand masher or electric mixer.

Meanwhile, while the potatoes are cooking, place the rest of the melted butter in the bottom of a skillet. Add the onions, carrots and celery. Sauté until carrots and other vegetables start to get tender; do not let burn. Add the remainder of the salt and pepper, peas, flour, beef broth and beef. Continue to heat until the beef begins to brown. Place in a lightly greased baking dish, pan or pie tin.

Spoon the mashed potatoes on top and bake for 30 minutes in a pre-heated, 350° degree oven (on the middle shelf). The potatoes will turn a light brown on top. Watch so they do not burn; in which case lower the heat and bake a little longer or place on a lower shelf.

An option would be to use a pie tin with an uncooked pastry shell.

CONTINENTAL SHEPHERD'S PIE

Ingredients to serve 4:

4 large potatoes, peeled and chunked
1/2 cup milk
1/2 stick butter, melted and divided
1 medium onion, peeled and broken into rings
1 cn. tomatoes, Italian style
2 ribs celery, chopped
1 pound seasoned pork sausage
1 t salt, divided
1/2 t pepper, divided
1 cup cheddar cheese, grated or shredded
1 unbaked, 9 inch pastry shell

Cover the potatoes with water in a sauce pan and boil (covered) 20 minutes or until done - test with a fork. Add the milk, half the melted butter, 1/2 t salt and 1/4 t pepper and mash with a hand masher or electric mixer.

Meanwhile, while the potatoes are cooking, place the rest of the butter in a skillet and add the onions, celery and the sausage (crumbled). Sauté about 5 minutes; stir and do not let burn.

Place the unbaked pastry shell in a pie tin. Pour the contents of the skillet into the shell.

Add the tomatoes, 1/2 t salt and 1/4 t pepper. Spoon the mashed potatoes on top; drizzle the remaining butter over the potatoes. Bake 30 minutes in a pre-heated 350° degree oven. The potatoes should brown slightly but do not let burn. If they start to burn, lower heat and place on a lower shelf.

After 30 minutes, sprinkle with grated cheese and return to oven until cheese is melted.

POTATO AND HAMBURGER PIE

Ingredients to serve 4:

4 large potatoes, peeled and chunked
1 pound lean ground beef
1 medium onion, chopped
2 ribs celery, chopped
1 cn. cream of mushroom soup
1/2 cup milk
1/2 stick butter or margarine, melted
1 t salt, divided
1/2 t pepper, divided
1 9 inch, unbaked pastry shell

Cover the potatoes with water in a sauce pan and boil (covered) 20 minutes or until done — test with a fork. Drain and return to the stove for a couple of minutes to dry the potatoes. Add the milk, 1/2 the melted butter, 1/2 t salt and 1/4 t pepper. Mash with a hand masher or electric mixer.

Meanwhile, while the potatoes are cooking, place the rest of the butter in a skillet and sauté the hamburger, onion and celery until the hamburger starts to turn brown (about 5 minutes). Stir in 1/2 t salt and 1/4 t pepper.

Place the pastry shell in the bottom of a pie tin. Transfer the ground beef, onions and celery (along with the melted butter) into the pie tin. Add the mushroom soup. Spoon the mashed potatoes on top. Drizzle the remaining butter over the potatoes. Bake in a pre-heated 350° oven for 30 minutes. Use the middle shelf. The potatoes should brown a little but do not let them burn. If they start to burn, use a lower shelf and/or reduce the heat.

MRS. OLSON'S POTATO CASSEROLE

Ingredients to serve 4-6:

1 32 oz. pkg. frozen, diced potatoes, thawed
1 16 oz. sour cream
1 cn. mushroom soup
1 cup cheddar cheese, shredded
seasoned salt

Mix sour cream with mushroom soup and cheese. Add potatoes and spread into a 13" x 9" lightly greased pan or baking dish. Sprinkle with seasoned salt. Cover and bake in a pre-heated 350° oven for 1 hour.

Courtesy Sharon Olson, Huntington Beach, California.

CHEESY VEGETABLE CASSEROLE

Ingredients to serve 6:

3 large potatoes, peeled and chunked bite-size
1 medium cabbage (about 2#), cut into bite-size chunks (discard core and outer portions)
1 large parsnip, peeled and sliced thin
1 large turnip, peeled and sliced thin
1 large carrot, peeled and sliced thin
1 medium rutabaga, peeled and diced
1 large onion, peeled, sliced and broken into rings
1/2 stick butter, melted and divided
1/2 t salt
1/4 t pepper
1-1/2 cups cheddar cheese, grated or shredded

Cover the potatoes, cabbage, carrot, rutabaga, turnip and parsnip pieces with water in a sauce pan and boil, covered, until the vegetables start to soften. Using a slotted spoon, remove the cabbage after 3 minutes, all of the vegetables except the potatoes after 5 minutes and remove the potatoes after 10 minutes.

Sauté the onion rings in a skillet in 1/2 of the butter.

Place all of the ingredients, including the melted butter, in a lightly greased baking dish or pan. Season with salt and pepper as you stir them together but save 1/2 cup of grated cheese to sprinkle on top. Bake in a pre-heated 350° oven covered, 1 hour.

TATER TOT CASSEROLE

Ingredients to serve 4-6:

1 32 oz. pkg. frozen Tater tots, thawed
1 pound lean ground beef
1 large onion, chopped
2 ribs celery, chopped
1 cn. French style green beans, drained
2 cns. cream of mushroom soup, undiluted
1/2 stick butter or margarine, melted
1 cn. French fried onions
1/2 t salt
1/4 t pepper

Sauté the onion and ground beef in the butter. Combine all of the ingredients except the French fried onion rings in a lightly greased casserole dish. Scatter the French fried onions over the top of the casserole. Cover, and bake for 1 hour in a pre-heated 375° oven. Uncover the casserole the last 15 minutes.

POTATO MUSHROOM CASSEROLE

Ingredients to serve 4:

4 large potatoes, sliced (peeling is optional)
1 pound fresh mushrooms or 8 oz. cn. mushrooms
1 medium onion, peeled and chopped
2 ribs celery, chopped
1 cn. mushroom soup
1 cup water
salt and pepper
1 cup bread crumbs or crushed corn flakes

Layer the sliced potatoes and mushrooms in a lightly greased casserole or flat baking dish. Scatter the celery and onions over-all. Combine the mushroom soup and the water and pour over the contents of the dish. Lightly season with the salt and pepper. Sprinkle the bread crumbs over-all. Bake in a pre-heated 350° degree oven for 1 hour or until potatoes are done.

Section VII
POTATO CAKES AND DUMPLINGS

MASHED POTATO PANCAKES

Ingredients for 6 cakes:

3 cups mashed potatoes

1/2 stick butter or margarine, melted

1/2 cup chopped chives

1 egg

2 T cooking oil

2 cloves garlic, peeled and minced

Sauté the garlic in the melted butter 3 or 4 minutes. Combine all ingredients including the butter used to sauté the garlic.

Spoon the potato mixture in 6 portions on a greased griddle or use a skillet. Flatten with a spatula into cakes. Fry over medium heat, brown on both sides.

Serve plain or with butter and/or sour cream.

POLISH POTATO PANCAKES

Ingredients to serve 6-8 cakes:

6 large potatoes, peeled and diced

1 small onion, peeled and diced

2 eggs

4 T flour

1/2 t salt

enough cooking oil so that it is about 1/2 inch deep in a skillet

Place the potatoes, onion and eggs in a blender until they have a "grated" appearance. Blend in the flour and salt. Pre-heat the oil in the skillet using a hot burner. Spoon the batter into the skillet, making 6-8 patties; flatten with a spatula. Fry until golden brown on both sides.

Serve plain or with butter and/or sour cream.

POTATO AND CHIVES CAKES

Ingredients to make 6 patties:

3 cups mashed potatoes
1/2 cup chopped chives
1 cup milk
1/2 cup sour cream
1/2 t salt
1 t pepper
1/2 stick butter, melted
enough cooking oil to make about 1/3 inch in a skillet

Combine all ingredients except the cooking oil and form into patties.
Fry in oil until a golden brown on both sides.
Serve plain or with butter and/or sour cream.

POTATO AND SALMON PATTIES

Ingredients for 6-8 patties:

3 cups mashed potatoes
1 pound pre-cooked salmon, deboned and flaked
2 T flour
1 T Worcestershire sauce
1 egg
1 cup water
1/2 T salt
1 T lemon pepper
1 cup cracker crumbs
enough oil to have 1/2 inch in a skillet

Combine all ingredients except the cracker crumbs and oil. Mix well.
Form into patties. Sprinkle both sides with cracker crumbs.
Pre-heat oil. Fry patties until a golden brown on both sides.

POTATO AND CARROT CAKES

Ingredients to make 8 patties:

2 cups grated potatoes
2 cups grated carrots
2 egg yolks
4 T butter
salt and pepper to taste

Combine all ingredients except butter and seasonings. Make into balls
and flatten with a spatula. Fry in a skillet in melted butter. Brown on
both sides and season to taste.

POTATO DUMPLINGS

Ingredients to make 12 dumplings:

3 cups raw potatoes, peeled and grated
3 cups mashed potatoes (use leftovers if you have them)
4 T flour
2 eggs
1 T corn starch
1 t salt

Mix together all ingredients. Meanwhile, start water boiling in a large soup kettle (about 3 quarts of water).

Make 1 dumpling—about the diameter of a half-dollar—and drop into the boiling water. If the dough starts to disintegrate, it means it is too soft. Add another T of cornstarch. Keep trying and adding cornstarch until the dumplings hold together. When it is the right consistency, make all of the dough into half-dollar size dumplings and drop them into the boiling water. Test after 5 minutes for doneness. May be served with butter or bacon bits or gravy.

ROSE GERMANN'S BASEBALL DUMPLINGS

Ingredients to serve 6 (as a side-dish):

6 large potatoes, peeled, quartered, cooked and mashed
4 slices toast (bite size pieces)
2 C flour
salt
1/4 pound butter, melted

Boil potatoes, mash and let cool. Using hands, mix potatoes and toast.Mix flour with potatoes to form a ball about the size of a baseball. You may need more flour. Put balls in boiling salted water for l5 to 20 minutes. When they float to the top, use a slotted spoon to take out. Brown butter and pour over balls.

Sometimes Rose would use l or 2 eggs and l t baking poowder.

In memory of Rose Germann, Staples, Minnesota.

CHARLES KING'S POTATO DUMPLINGS WITH HAM

Bake 1/2 cross cut ham, fully cooked, for 2 hours in a covered roaster. Place the ham on a shallow rack, cut side down. Add 2 inches of water. Optional: after cooking for 1-1/2 hours pour 1 can of beer over ham and resume cooking for 30 minutes. Remove ham and cool before slicing. Cool broth overnight by pouring into kettle and refrigerating or placing roaster in garage (if winter time).

Next morning skim off the white fat from the broth. Pour broth into 3 or 4 quart kettle and add 2 quarts of water. Kettle size is large, but that makes cooking the dumplings easier.

Making the Dumplings

Peel 8 medium sized potatoes. Cut the potatoes, by hand, into smaller pieces and then chop in food processor into a grated texture, using large chopping blade. Drain off excessive juice or pat off juice with paper towel. This will cause you to use less flour when making the dumplings, and the dumplings will be lighter.

Place grated potatoes in a large mixing bowl. Add one egg, 2/3 tsp. baking powder and 1 tablespoon of salt. Mix and add enough flour so mixture can be made into medium to large dumplings, using a large mixing spoon.

Boiling Dumplings

Bring ham broth to a boil. Dip mixing spoon into broth as you form the dumplings—put in broth and lift dumplings from the bottom of the spoon until they float to the top.

Important

Don't overcook. In about 3-4 minutes, remove and cut one dumpling in half. When done, the center of the dumpling should look porous. If you overcook the dumplings, the centers will get hard and look glazed. Proper cooking of the dumplings is the key to making good dumplings. DON'T OVERCOOK THEM!!!

Courtesy Charles King, Grand Forks, North Dakota.

Section VIII
MISCELLANEOUS RECIPES

BOILED POTATOES

There are many people who prefer to eat boiled potatoes just as they are rather than mash or rice them. There is a difference in flavor.

Small, new potatoes are usually boiled whole, with skins on. Larger potatoes are usually peeled and chunked.

Here are a few variations:

1. With dill -

Boil a few sprigs of dill along with the potatoes. Serve with a generous amount of melted butter and garnish with chopped fresh dill (not the same as boiled with the potatoes - discard the boiled dill.)

2. With cream and dill -

Save 1 cup of the water in which the potatoes were boiled. Discard the rest of the water. Into this cup of reserved liquid, whisk 4 T melted butter or margarine and 3 T flour.

Return the potatoes to the sauce pan along with the water-flour-butter mixture. Bring to a boil, then reduce heat and simmer until the sauce begins to thicken – stirring all the while.

When the sauce starts to thicken, add 1/2 cup of heavy cream. Continue stirring and heating a few more minutes.

Garnish with 3 T chopped, fresh dill and salt and pepper to taste.

3. With a white sauce -

Make a white sauce by whisking together 2 T melted butter, 2 T flour, 1 cup milk, 1/2 t salt and 1/4 t pepper. Cook until thick, stirring continually.

4. With parsley -

Drizzle generous amounts of butter over the potatoes and sprinkle with chopped, fresh parsley.

5. With chive and milk gravy -

Prepare a gravy of 2 cups of milk (no less than 2%) or half and half and 4 T fresh chopped chives.

BOILED POTATOES WITH CREAM AND DILL

Ingredients to serve 4:

12 to 16 (depending on size) small new potatoes
2 T butter, melted
2 T flour
4 T heavy cream
2 T fresh dill, chopped
salt and pepper to taste

In a sauce pan, cover the potatoes with water, cover, boil about 10-15 minutes. Check occasionally with a fork; don't let potatoes get mushy.
Drain the potatoes, saving 1 cup of the liquid. Whisk together this cup of liquid with the flour and butter.
Return the potatoes to the sauce pan along with the water-flour-butter mixture. Stir and simmer until sauce begins to thicken. Stir in cream. Continue heating and stirring 2 or 3 more minutes.
Salt and pepper to taste.
Garnish with chopped dill.

NEW POTATOES WITH JUNE PEAS

Ingredients to serve 6:

2 pounds new miniature red potatoes, skins on or off
1-1/2 cups small, early June peas, fresh or frozen
salt and pepper to taste
1/4 pound (1 stick) butter or margarine

Boil the potatoes until done; test with a fork. Let cool to room temperature.
Melt the butter in a skillet and sauté the potatoes and peas until piping hot.
Season to taste.

POTATOES IN FOIL
(IN THE OVEN OR ON THE GRILL)

Ingredients to serve 6:

6 medium to large potatoes, peeled and sliced
1 large onion, peeled, sliced and broken into rings
1/2 cup shredded cheddar cheese
1/4 pound (1 stick) butter or margarine
2 T steak sauce of your choosing
salt and pepper to taste (easy on the salt; generous with the pepper)

Place the sliced potatoes on heavy foil (no more than 2 layers)
Scatter the onion rings over the potatoes.
Scatter the cheese and pats of butter over-all. Sprinkle the steak sauce over-all. Season with salt and pepper.
Fold the foil over contents, sealing with your fingers. Bake in a 350° degree oven or closed grill for 30-40 minutes or until potatoes are soft.

FRENCH FRIES

These are just a few basic rules for good French Fries:

1. Use a good quality potato - fresh and hard.
2. Discard any that have dark spots.
3. Use fresh oil (I like peanut oil best) Strain it through a fairly fine sieve if you are going to use it more than once.

FRENCH FRIES IN BATTER

For a delightful variation prepare a light pancake batter (I use the "complete" package mixes and just add water) and dip the fries either raw or frozen into the batter and then drop them into hot oil.

OVEN-BAKED POTATO CHIPS

Ingredients to serve 8:

8 large potatoes, peeled and sliced very thin
1 stick butter or margarine (1/4 pound) melted
salt and pepper to taste
options: 3 T herbs, parsley flakes, chopped chives, rosemary, thyme, etc.

Peel and slice the potatoes (about 1/8 inch thick).
Pre-heat the oven to 500° degrees.
Lightly grease 2 cookie sheets. Arrange the potato slices in a single layer. Brush chips with butter. Sprinkle lightly with salt, pepper and other herbs.
Bake on the middle rack 6 minutes. If the chips appear to be browning more on one of the trays than the other, turn the trays. Continue to bake another 7 or 8 minutes or until chips appear browned around the edges.

FINNAN HADDIE

Ingredients to serve 4:

4 large potatoes, peeled and chunked bite-size
1 pound white meat fish fillets, baked or poached and flaked into small pieces
1 cn. cream of celery or cream of onion soup
1 cup milk
4 pats of butter
salt and pepper to taste
garnish with parsley flakes or chopped dill

Cover the potatoes with water in a sauce pan and boil, covered, for about 20 minutes or until done - check with a fork.

Meanwhile, bake or poach the fish and break into small pieces.

Combine all of the ingredients, except the butter, in a sauce pan and bring to a boil, then reduce heat and let simmer about 5 minutes or until well heated.

Put one pat of butter on each serving. Garnish with parsley flakes or chopped dill.

SCANDINAVIAN HERRING AND POTATOES

Ingredients to serve 4:

1 cup pickled herring, chopped very fine
2 cups small boiled potatoes, sliced thin
4 slices rye bread, buttered
enough leaf lettuce to cover bread

Butter the bread, top with lettuce, then potato slices, then herring. Mayonnaise may be used instead of butter.

POTATO LATKES #1
(A TRADITIONAL JEWISH DELICACY)

Ingredients for about 24 potato pancakes:

4 medium potatoes, grated (russets work well)
1 medium onion, chopped fine
3 T matzo meal (you may substitute all purpose flour)
1 egg, beaten
1/2 t salt
1/2 t pepper
oil

Combine all of the ingredients in a bowl. Place a generous amount of oil (about 1 inch) in an iron skillet and heat (medium). When it is hot, drop 1 T of the mixture into the oil. It will tend to flatten out. If the mixture does not hold together, add a little milk to the mixture. Cook until a golden brown, turning once. This should take about 3 minutes on each side.

Serve with any of the following: smoked fish, caviar, apple sauce, sour cream or yogurt.

POTATO LATKES #2
(WITH APPLE)

Ingredients for about 1 dozen pancakes:
(a slightly different recipe)

2 cups grated or finely chopped potatoes

1 cup grated or finely chopped apple (no peel or core)

4 T flour

1 egg

1/2 t salt

1/2 t pepper

oil for frying

Combine grated apple and potato; add and stir in all other ingredients. Pre-heat a generous amount of oil (about 1/4 inch) in a heavy skillet so that the oil is ready when you finish mixing the batter. Using a tablespoon, drop 3 spoonfuls per pancake into the hot oil. Allow about 3 minutes to brown on bottom side, then turn with a spatula; fry until brown on both sides. If the batter is so thick that it does not flatten out on its own when dropped in the oil, gently flatten with a spatula. Option: sprinkle with confectionery sugar.

ROLLED POTATO BALLS

Ingredients to serve 4:

3 medium red potatoes - peeled and quartered

1/4 cup grated Parmesan cheese

1-1/2 cup Phil. Cream cheese

1 T butter

2-1/2 t instant onion soup mix

1 T chopped green onion

1 beaten egg

dash of pepper

1-1/2 cups crushed corn flakes

1-2 T milk (see below)

Cook potatoes until tender, drain and mash. Stir in Parmesan cheese, cream cheese, butter, onions, soup mix and seasoning. Add 1-2 T milk if mixture is dry. Shape mixture into 8 balls. Dip in beaten egg. Roll in corn flakes. Place on greased baking sheet. Bake at 400° degrees—10-15 minutes or until hot and crispy.

Courtesy Dorothy Liljegren, Hot Springs, Arkansas.

POTATO LEFSE

Ingredients for 8 to 10 – 14 inch lefsas:

Peel and boil as many potatoes as you need (figuring 1 medium potato for each lefsa you plan to make). When potatoes are done, drain and add a little milk and 1/4 pound of butter and mash well. For 8 to 10 - 14 inch lefsas you will need:

3 cups mashed potatoes

1 cup flour

1/4 cup heavy cream

1 T sugar

Mix together all ingredients (like pie crust). Form into 8 to 10 parts and roll thin. Bake on lefsa grill until brown; turn and bake on the other side.

Courtesy Arvis Sandland, Clearbrook, Minnesota.

POTATO SOUP WITH SALMON

Ingredients to sere 4:

2/3 cup instant potatoes

1 small cn. Salmon

1 medium onion, peeled and chopped

1 cn. chicken broth or fish stock

1 2 oz. jar pimentos, chopped

salt and pepper to taste

Prepare the mashed potatoes according to directions on the box. Combine all ingredients in a soup pot; bring to a boil; then reduce to simmer and cook for 15 minutes.

POTATO SAUSAGE (POTATIS KORV)
A SCANDINAVIAN FAVORITE

3 pounds ground pork (lean)

2 pound lean ground beef

10 pounds potatoes

2 T pepper

5 T salt

1-1/2 t allspice (ground)

1-1/2 t ginger

1/2 pound casings

Soak casings in water to soften and remove salt. Peel and grind potatoes, using medium blade. Add meat and seasonings. Mix well. Tie end of casing and loosely fill in 24" lengths—tie open ends. (The sausage expands when cooked). Keep covered with water. Prick in several places before cooking. Simmer for 30-45 minutes. Drain off water and sauté slowly until browned.

Uncooked potato sausage may be frozen in airtight zip-locked bags. Exposure to air causes the potatoes to discolor.

Courtesy Karen Anderson Cowie, Gull Lake, Minnesota.

HOT *(IN MORE WAYS THAN ONE!)* POTATO SKINS

Ingredients to serve 4:

Skins from 4 large baked potatoes
1 pound lean ground beef
1 cn. chili beans
1 cn. tomatoes (Mexican style)
2 ribs celery, chopped
1 medium onion, peeled and chopped
1 t chili powder or to taste
1 t ground cumin
3 T cooking oil

Brown the hamburger, onion and celery in the oil.
Meanwhile, brown the potato skins on a cookie sheet in a 400° degree oven.
Add the kidney beans, tomato sauce and seasonings to the skillet and cook over medium heat until piping hot.
Serve the chili in the potato skins—2 skins per serving.

POTATO CAKE

Ingredients to serve 4:

4 large potatoes, peeled, boiled and grated
1 small onion, peeled and chopped
2 T cooking oil, divided
2 T butter, melted, divided

Peel the potatoes and cut them in half. Cook them in boiling water, covered for about 20 minutes or until done — test with a fork. Let cool. Grate them, using a hand grater. Combine with the chopped onion and season to taste with salt and pepper. Using a skillet about the size where the potato-onion mixture will be about 3/4 of an inch thick, heat (medium) 1 T oil and 1 T butter; add the potato-onion mixture and press level with a spatula. Fry until brown on the under-side. Turn out on a plate and then return to the skillet raw side down. After adding another 1 T oil and 1 T butter to the skillet, fry until that side is also brown. Cut into 4 slices with a knife and serve with a spatula.

POTATO FISH

You won't believe this until you try it.

4 fresh fillets (any fish including catfish and bullheads)
1 beaten egg
1 cup instant mashed potato flakes
1 envelope onion salad dressing mix
salad oil

Season fish with salt and pepper. Combine egg and 1 T water. Combine potato flakes and dressing mix. Dip fish into egg mixture, then roll in potato mixture. Repeat. Brown fish in hot salad oil on one side for 4 to 5 minutes. Turn carefully and brown second side. Drain on paper toweling.

POTATO PIZZA

Ingredients:

1 pkg. Pizza dough
2 cups shredded cheese (combine several varieties)
2 large potatoes, cooked, peeled and sliced thin
1 T garlic salt
2 T olive oil

Press pizza dough onto a lightly greased cookie sheet into a circle. Bake about 6 minutes in a pre-heated 400° degree oven. Brush generously with olive oil. Sprinkle with garlic salt. Sprinkle with half the cheeses. Arrange the sliced, cooked potatoes over the cheese; overlap the slices if that is necessary to fit them all in. Sprinkle with remainder of garlic salt. Top with the rest of the cheeses. Return to the oven for about 12 minutes or until the crust is brown.

POTATO TORTILLA

Ingredients to serve 4:

1 cup mashed potatoes
4 T chopped onion
1 clove garlic, minced
4 T chopped mushrooms of your choosing
2 T grated or shredded cheese of your choosing
3 T olive oil or cooking oil
3 large eggs
1 cup chopped, cooked spinach (frozen or fresh)
salt and pepper to taste

Sauté the onion and garlic in 1 T oil until onion is "clear".

Add potatoes, spinach, mushrooms and cheese to skillet and cook over medium heat until warm throughout.

In a bowl, lightly beat the eggs. Dump the contents of the skillet into the bowl and thoroughly stir together.

Add another T of oil to the skillet and transfer the contents of the bowl to the skillet. Increase the heat a bit. As the mixture solidifies you will be able to "swirl" the tortilla round in the pan. When the underside is a golden brown, turn it on to a plate with the cooked side up. Add the remainder of the oil to the skillet and slide the tortilla back into the skillet, cooked side still up. Continue to cook and swirl until bottom side is also a golden brown.

Cut with a knife into 4 pieces and serve with a spatula.

Option: hot sauce or salsa on the side.

MASHED POTATO DONUTS

Ingredients:

4 T butter
1 cup hot mashed potatoes
3 eggs
1-1/4 cup sugar
1 cup milk
4 cups flour
6 t baking powder
1 t salt
1/2 t vanilla
vegetable oil

Add butter to potatoes and beat well. Beat eggs with sugar and stir into potatoes. Add remaining ingredients except vegetable oil. Mix well. Let stand in a cold place 1 hour.

In a deep fryer, heat about 4 inches of vegetable oil until very hot. On a lightly floured board, roll out the dough to about 1/4 inch thickness. (The dough may take a little more flour). Cut out with donut cutter and drop into hot oil. Cook until golden brown. Drain on brown paper bags. Serve warm. May be shaken in cinnamon sugar or powdered sugar.

Courtesy Northern Lights, Beltrami Electric Coop.

Section IX
SWEET POTATOES

REALLY SWEET, SWEET POTATOES

Ingredients to serve 6:

6 medium sweet potatoes, cooked, peeled and mashed
1 cup crushed pineapple, undrained
1 cup brown sugar, packed
1 cup pecans, crushed (coarse)
marshmallows

Thoroughly mix together the mashed sweet potatoes, pineapple and brown sugar. Lightly grease a baking dish with butter. Spoon the sweet potato mixture into the baking dish and level surface with the spoon or a spatula. Dot surface with as many marshmallows as you like.
Bake in a medium oven about 30 minutes or until heated throughout and marshmallows turn brown.

SWEET POTATO DISKS

Peel and slice sweet potatoes into discs about 1 inch thick. Brush with olive oil or place in a plastic bag with olive oil for a short time (turning over ever so often). Lay on a baking sheet. Sprinkle with salt and pepper or seasonings of choice. Bake in a pre-heated 400° degree oven for 20 minutes or until tender. Turn over once during baking.

Courtesy Betsy Hayenga, Cushing, Minnesota

MAPLE FLAVORED SWEET POTATOES

Ingredients to serve 6:

2 cns. sweet potatoes (16 oz.) The equivalent would be about 6 good size potatoes, peeled and cooked
1/2 stick butter or margarine, melted
2/3 cup maple syrup
4 T brown sugar
1/2 t nutmeg

Place the cooked sweet potatoes in a lightly greased baking dish. Use a dish large enough so that the potatoes cover the bottom of the dish and are just touching.

Place the butter, sugar, syrup and nutmeg in a sauce pan. Bring to a boil, then reduce heat to simmer and cook for 5 minutes. Pour over the potatoes and bake in a pre-heated medium oven for 30 minutes.

SWEET POTATOES WITH APPLES

Ingredients to serve 6:

6 large sweet potatoes, peeled and sliced thick (about 1 inch)

4 large hard apples (like Winesap or Prairie Spy)

3 T cinnamon

1/2 cup brown sugar

Begin with a layer of sweet potatoes in a lightly greased casserole or baking dish. Core, peel and slice the apples. Arrange in a layer over the potatoes. Sprinkle generously with cinnamon and brown sugar. Bake in a pre-heated 350° degree oven covered–or use foil–for 1 hour or until potatoes are tender.

SWEET POTATOES IN WINE

Ingredients to serve 6:

2 16 oz. cns. sweet potatoes

1 cup white wine

8 slices bacon, fried crisp and crumbled

Arrange the potatoes on the bottom of a lightly greased baking dish. Pour the wine over the potatoes. Sprinkle with crumbled bacon.

Bake in a covered dish (foil will work) in a pre-heated 350° degree oven for 40 minutes.

SWEET POTATOES WITH BRANDY AND NUTS

Ingredients to serve 6:

2 16 oz. cns. sweet potatoes

4 T brandy*

1 cup pecans, crushed coarse

2 T brown sugar

1/2 stick butter, melted

Mash together all ingredients. Bake in a lightly greased, covered baking dish in a pre-heated medium oven for 40 minutes.

*may substitute bourbon

SWEET AND SOUR SWEET POTATOES

Ingredients to serve 6:

6 medium-large sweet potatoes
1 cup sour cream
4 T chopped chives
salt and pepper to taste

Bake the potatoes in a pre-heated 350° degree oven for 45 minutes or until done–test with a fork.
Let cool and peel. Mash together all ingredients. Spoon into a lightly greased baking dish and re-heat in a medium oven for about 35 minutes or until piping hot.

SWEET POTATOES WITH PECANS
AND A TOUCH OF ORANGE

Ingredients to serve 6:

6 sweet potatoes baked, peeled and mashed or 2 - 16 oz. cans
2 T grated orange peel
1/2 cup orange juice
1-1/2 cups chopped pecans
1/2 cup brown sugar
salt and pepper to taste

Combine all ingredients and place in a lightly greased casserole or baking dish and bake in a pre-heated 350° degree oven for about 25 minutes or until piping hot.

MELLOW SWEET POTATOES

Ingredients to serve 6:

6 large sweet potatoes, cooked and mashed or 2 - 16 oz. cans
1/2 cup milk
1/2 stick butter or margarine, melted
4 eggs, beaten
1 t nutmeg
1/2 t salt
top with lots of marshmallows

Combine all ingredients, thoroughly. Place in a lightly greased casserole or baking dish. Top with marshmallows. Bake in a pre-heated 350° degree oven for 25 minutes or until piping hot.

SWEET POTATO WEDGES

Ingredients to serve 4:

4 large sweet potatoes, cut in half (lengthwise) and then cross-wise into wedges
1 t cinnamon
1/2 cup orange juice
1/2 cup cranberry juice
1 T cooking oil

Place the last four ingredients in a bowl; toss the wedges in the liquid until well-coated. Save the liquid. Arrange the wedges on a cookie sheet and bake in a pre-heated 400° degree oven for about 40 minutes or until wedges are a little crisp but not soft.

Sprinkle with remaining juices a couple of times while baking.

SWEET POTATO FRENCH FRIES

Ingredients to serve 4:

4 large yams or sweet potatoes, peeled and cut into French fry strips
4 T olive oil
2 T Parmesan cheese
2 t seasoned salt
1/2 t pepper

Place all ingredients in a plastic bag and shake vigorously.

Spray a large cookie sheet with shortening. Arrange fries on sheet in a single layer without touching. Bake in a pre-heated 450° degree oven for 15 minutes; turn after 7 or 8 minutes.

Courtesy Sue Eddy, Staples, Minnesota.

SWEET POTATOES WITH CHEESE

Ingredients to serve 4:

4 large sweet potatoes, cooked and mashed
1 egg, lightly beaten
1 cup cream
1/2 t salt
grated Parmesan cheese

Combine first 4 ingredients, thoroughly. Place in a lightly greased casserole dish and bake, covered in a pre-heated 350° degree oven for 20 minutes. Sprinkle cheese generously over surface and continue to bake, uncovered, for another 15 minutes.

SENATOR RICHARD RUSSEL'S SWEET POTATOES

Ingredients to serve 4:

4 cups cooked, mashed sweet potatoes

3/4 cup granulated sugar

2 eggs, lightly beaten

1 T vanilla extract

2/3 cup milk

2/3 cup butter, melted

Put ingredients (thoroughly mixed) into a buttered casserole dish. Top with the following mixture and bake about 45 minutes in a pre-heated 350° degree oven:

3/4 cup brown sugar

1/3 cup flour

1/3 cup butter, melted

Russel was a distinguished United States Senator from Georgia
who served during the mid 1900s

SWEET POTATO STRIPS WITH LIME

Ingredients to serve 4:

4 large sweet potatoes

4 limes

4 cups vegetable oil

sprinkle with salt

Peel the sweet potatoes. Cut lengthwise into strips (resembling French fries only longer).

Pre-heat the oil in a heavy skillet to about 400° degrees. Fry the strips in batches. They should turn brown and crisp in a couple of minutes. Remove with a slotted spoon. Place on a paper towel to drain. Sprinkle with salt and lemon juice.

SWEET POTATO PECAN PIE

Ingredients:

1 unbaked pie shell

3 cups mashed sweet potatoes

2 eggs, beaten

1 cup cream

1/2 cup brown sugar

3 T butter, melted

1-1/2 cups pecans, chopped

Combine sweet potatoes, cream and eggs; stir together until smooth.
Spoon into the pie shell. Bake in a pre-heated 375° degree oven for 45
minutes.
Sprinkle the brown sugar, pecans and melted butter over the surface.
Option: top with whipped cream.

SWEET POTATOES WITH BACON

Ingredients to serve 6:

6 sweet potatoes, peeled and chunked
10 slices bacon, fried crisp and broken into bits
1/2 stick butter or margarine, melted
1/2 cup white wine
1/2 cup brown sugar

Fry and crumble the bacon and set aside.
Peel and cut the sweet potatoes into chunks.
Using a lightly buttered casserole dish, place the sweet potatoes on the
bottom and then sprinkle with the wine, melted butter and brown
sugar. Place in a pre-heated 350° degree oven for 30 to 40 minutes or
until the sweet potatoes are soft. Add the bacon bits and mash
everything together.

SWEET POTATO SOUP

Ingredients to serve 6:

3 large sweet potatoes
1 carrot, scraped and sliced
1 rib celery, chopped
1 onion, chopped
1 cn. lima beans, drained
1 t garlic salt
1 T brown sugar
1 t cinnamon
4 cups water
add pepper to taste
parsley for garnish

Combine all ingredients in a soup pot. Bring to a boil, then reduce heat
to simmer and cook for 40 minutes or until all vegetables are tender.
Option: let cool and purée in batches and re-heat.
Add parsley for garnish.

Other Books by Duane R. Lund

Andrew, Youngest Lumberjack
A Beginner's Guide to Hunting and Trapping
A Kid's Guidebook to Fishing Secrets
Early Native American Recipes and Remedies
Fishing and Hunting Stories from The Lake of the Woods
Lake of the Woods, Yesterday and Today, Vol. 1
Lake of the Woods, Earliest Accounts, Vol. 2
Our Historic Boundary Waters
Our Historic Upper Mississippi
Tales of Four Lakes and a River
The Youngest Voyageur
White Indian Boy
Nature's Bounty for Your Table
The North Shore of Lake Superior, Yesterday and Today
Leech Lake, Yesterday and Today
Gull Lake, Yesterday and Today
101 Favorite Freshwater Fish Recipes
101 Favorite Wild Rice Recipes
101 Favorite Mushroom Recipes
Camp Cooking, Made Easy and Fun
Sauces, Seasonings and Marinades for Fish and Wild Game
The Scandinavian Cookbook
Gourmet Freshwater Fish Recipes, Quick and Easy
The Soup Cookbook
101 Ways to Add to Your Income
The Indian Wars
Traditional Holiday Ethnic Recipes - collected all over the world
Entertainment Helpers, Quick and Easy

About the Author

- EDUCATOR (RETIRED, SUPERINTENDENT OF SCHOOLS, STAPLES, MINNESOTA);
- HISTORIAN (PAST MEMBER OF EXECUTIVE BOARD, MINNESOTA HISTORICAL SOCIETY); Past Member of BWCA and National Wilderness Trails Advisory Committees;
- SENIOR CONSULTANT to the Blandin Foundation
- WILDLIFE ARTIST, OUTDOORSMAN.